ONE WORD Substitutions

ONE WORD Substitutions

Roshan Tolani

arihant
Arihant Publications (India) Limited

Arihant Publications (India) Ltd.

卐 Administrative & Production Offices

Regd. Office
'Ramchhaya' 4577/15, Agarwal Road, Darya Ganj, New Delhi -110002
Tele: 011- 47630600, 43518550; Fax: 011- 23280316

Head Office
Kalindi, TP Nagar, Meerut (UP) - 250002
Tele: 0121-2401479, 2512970, 4004199; Fax: 0121-2401648

卐 Sales & Support Offices

Agra, Ahmedabad, Bengaluru, Bhubaneswar, Bareilly, Chennai, Delhi, Guwahati, Hyderabad, Jaipur, Jhansi, Kolkata, Lucknow, Meerut, Nagpur & Pune

卐 ISBN : 978-93-13160-19-9

卐 Price : ₹ 90.00

PO No. : TXT-59-T066783-08-25

PUBLISHED BY ARIHANT PUBLICATIONS (INDIA) LTD.

For further information about books Published by Arihant log on to www.arihantbooks.com or email to info@arihantbooks.com

PREFACE

The book One Word Substitutions is a kind of a reverse dictionary. The examiners use this test to evaluate the students' command over English vocabulary. In this type of questions, the students taking the verbal ability test are required to answer by writing a single word which can be used appropriately in place of the given description.

Knowledge of One Word Substitutes helps the students not only in scoring well in exams but also in achieving excellent proficiency in English language.

Often, learners of English use vague words and long sentences. English is a rich language and has a large number of words. By substituting verbose sentences with precise words, one can convey one's ideas more clearly.

The present book is a fairly good collection of One Word Substitutes. Though it is not an exhaustive list, it is certainly an honest effort to explain highly useful words. It includes words and definitions which are often asked in national and international competitive and entrance examinations. Moreover, the knowledge of these words will also help the students and learners of English to enhance their writing, speaking and reading skills.

I hope the book will prove very useful to all the learners of English. Any suggestion for improvement of the book will be highly appreciated.

Roshan Tolani

CONTENTS

✠ A judge's private room, without the press or the public being present	**In camera**
✠ A period of time in the past that was idyllically happy and peaceful	**Halcyon**
✠ A tax or levy	**Cess**
✠ An abbreviation formed from the initial letters of other words and pronounced as a word	**Acronym**
✠ An ability to do several things at the same time	**Multitasking**
✠ An ability to express oneself well in speech	**Oracy**
✠ An ability to make good judgements and take quick decisions	**Acumen**
✠ An ability to see what will or might happen in the future	**Foresight**
✠ An ability to stay calm in difficult or dangerous situations	**Sangfroid**
✠ An ability to use one's hands skilfully or an ability to think quickly and effectively	**Dexterity**
✠ An ability, talent, or special skill needed to do something	**Knack**
✠ Able to become strong, healthy, or successful again after something bad happens	**Resilient**
✠ Able to do many different things	**Versatile**
✠ Able to exist together without trouble or conflict; going together well	**Compatible**
✠ Acceptable according to the law, fair or reasonable	**Valid**
✠ Accepting and closely following the traditional beliefs and customs of a religion	**Orthodox**
✠ An act of burying a dead person	**Interment**

- ✠ An act of carefully watching someone or something especially in order to prevent or detect a crime — **Surveillance**
- ✠ An act of causing two people or groups to become friendly again after an argument or disagreement — **Reconciliation**
- ✠ An act of committing a serious crime such as murder or rape — **Felony**
- ✠ An act of destroying or damaging something deliberately so that it does not work correctly — **Sabotage**
- ✠ An act of ending the employment of a worker or group of workers — **Layoff**
- ✠ An act of explaining something — **Exposition**
- ✠ An act of getting money back from people it has been paid to — **Clawback**
- ✠ An act of going or travelling to a place along a way that is different from the usual or planned way — **Detour**
- ✠ An act of identifying a disease, illness, or problem by examining someone or something — **Diagnosis**
- ✠ An act of illegally copying someone's product or invention without permission — **Piracy**
- ✠ An act of no longer caring for, using, or doing something, failure to do one's job or duty — **Dereliction**
- ✠ An act of officially charging someone with a crime — **Indictment**
- ✠ An act of printing a statement about somebody that is not true and that gives people a bad opinion of him/her — **Libel**
- ✠ An act of punishing or harming somebody in return for what he/she has done to you, your family or friends — **Vengeance**
- ✠ An act of remembering or telling about past experiences — **Reminiscence**
- ✠ An act of returning something that was lost or stolen to its owner — **Restitution**
- ✠ An act of sending someone to another person or place for treatment, help, advice, etc. — **Referral**

✠ An act of treating a holy place or object in a way that does not show proper respect	**Sacrilege**
✠ An act of trying to impress someone by saying the names of well-known people that one knows or has met	**Name-dropping**
✠ An act or fact of having a romantic or sexual relationship with someone other than one's husband, wife, or partner	**Infidelity**
✠ An act or means of sealing off a place to prevent goods or people from entering or leaving	**Blockade**
✠ An act or remark that is calculated to gain an advantage	**Gambit**
✠ An act that is part of a usually religious ceremony	**Rite**
✠ An act, activity, or process of finding the way to get to a place when one is travelling in a ship, airplane, car	**Navigation**
✠ An action of making amends for a wrong or injury	**Atonement**
✠ An action of marrying a person of a superior caste or class	**Hypergamy**
✠ An action of regaining or gaining possession of something in exchange for payment, or clearing a debt	**Redemption**
✠ An action or event that is a signal for somebody to do something	**Cue**
✠ An action or offence of speaking sacrilegiously about God or sacred things; profane talk	**Blasphemy**
✠ An activity or art of copying the behaviour or speech of other people	**Mimicry**
✠ An activity or excitement that is unusual and that often is not wanted or necessary	**Fuss**
✠ An activity in that more and more people are becoming involved	**Bandwagon**
✠ Actor or actress	**Thespian**
✠ Add notes (to a text or diagram) giving explanation or comment	**Annotate**

✠ An additional fact or piece of information about a story that occurs after the main part	**Postscript**
✠ Advantages or gains secured as a result of corrupt practices	**Graft**
✠ An advice and future prediction based on the date of a person's birth and the positions of the stars and planets	**Horoscope**
✠ Agreed to by everyone	**Unanimous**
✠ An agreement between enemies or opponents to stop fighting, arguing, etc, for a certain period of time	**Truce**
✠ An alcoholic liquor especially when it is cheap or made illegally	**Hooch**
✠ All the plants that live in a particular area, time, period, or environment	**Flora**
✠ All the things that a person is able to do	**Repertoire**
✠ Allowed to know about something secret	**Privy**
✠ Always or often happening or existing	**Inveterate**
✠ An amount (such as an amount of money) that is more than the amount that is needed	**Surplus**
✠ An amount of money given to a retiring soldier or employee	**Gratuity**
✠ An amount of money paid for a service	**Honorarium**
✠ An amount of money that a company or the government pays to a person who is old or sick and no longer works	**Pension**
✠ An amount of money that is given to someone in return for providing help in a secret and dishonest business deal	**Kickback**
✠ An amount of money that is paid at one time	**Lump sum**
✠ An amount of money that is spent	**Outlay**
✠ An amount of money that must be paid and that is collected by a government or other authority	**Levy**
✠ An amount of something that is produced by a person or thing	**Output**

- ✠ An amount of time that a person holds a job, office, or title **Tenure**
- ✠ Amusing and very strange **Wacky**
- ✠ An angry and unpleasant woman, sexually attractive woman **Vixen**
- ✠ An argument that is complicated and continues over a long period of time **Wrangle**
- ✠ An invigilator at a university or college examination **Proctor**
- ✠ An ancient text in the form of a book; official list of medicines or chemicals **Codex**
- ✠ Anger caused by something that is unfair or wrong **Indignation**
- ✠ An angry and usually long speech or piece of writing that strongly criticizes someone or something **Diatribe**
- ✠ An angry woman who often complains about and criticises other people **Virago**
- ✠ An animal or plant that lives in or on another animal or plant and gets food or protection from it **Parasite**
- ✠ An animal that has four feet **Quadruped**
- ✠ Annoy (someone) by often complaining about his or her behaviour, appearance **Nag**
- ✠ Annoyance or distress at having failed or been humiliated **Chagrin**
- ✠ An annual calendar containing important dates and statistical information such as astronomical data and tide tables **Almanac**
- ✠ Any one of the large parts that some countries are divided into **Province**
- ✠ Any one of the lines that go from the North Pole to the South Pole on maps of the world **Meridian**
- ✠ Appearing, happening, or arriving soon **Forthcoming**
- ✠ An area around or near a particular place **Vicinity**
- ✠ An area in a desert where there is water and plants **Oasis**

- ✠ An area of land that has a particular quality or appearance — **Landscape**
- ✠ An area of sea water that is separated from the ocean by a reef or sandbar — **Lagoon**
- ✠ An area of soft, wet ground; situation that is hard to deal with or get out of — **Quagmire**
- ✠ An area that is not close to any cities or towns — **Hinterland**
- ✠ An area with people who are different in some way from the people in the areas around it — **Enclave**
- ✠ An area within which someone or something has authority, influence, or knowledge — **Purview**
- ✠ Argue loudly about things that are not important — **Squabble**
- ✠ Argue with someone in a friendly way — **Spar**
- ✠ An arrangement of events or dates in the order of their occurrence — **Chronology**
- ✠ An arrangement of leaves, flowers, fruits, etc, in the shape of a circle that is used for decoration — **Wreath**
- ✠ An arrangement to meet somebody at a particular time and place — **Rendezvous**
- ✠ Arrival of a large number of people — **Influx**
- ✠ An art of growing ornamental, artificially dwarfed varieties of trees and shrubs in pots — **Bonsai**
- ✠ An art, science, or profession of teaching — **Pedagogy**
- ✠ As compared with; as opposed to — **Vis-à-vis**
- ✠ Asking for or demanding and taking (something) for one's use — **Requisition**
- ✠ At or near the end of a piece of writing — **Ad fin**
- ✠ Attacking on the reputation and integrity of someone or something — **Aspersion**
- ✠ Attractive in a sexual way with large breasts and hips — **Voluptuous**
- ✠ An attractively arranged bunch of flowers, especially one presented as a gift or carried at a ceremony — **Bouquet**
- ✠ Average or ordinary — **Run-of-the-mill**

✠ Back in which the spine is curved in an abnormal way	**Hunchback**
✠ Bad or immoral behaviour or habits	**Vice**
✠ Bad or immoral behaviour that involves sex, drugs, alcohol, etc	**Debauchery**
✠ Bad or unfavourable; not good	**Untoward**
✠ Based on random choices or personal whims, rather than any reason or system	**Arbitrary**
✠ Based on what is known or seen when something is first considered or dealt with	**Prima facie**
✠ Basic equipment and structures (such as roads and bridges) that are needed for a country, region, or organisation to function properly	**Infrastructure**
✠ Be a sign of (something that is beginning to happen or will happen soon)	**Herald**
✠ Be angry or upset about something and to refuse to discuss it with other people	**Sulk**
✠ Be deprived of a close relation or friend through their death	**Bereave**
✠ Be repeated several times as it is reflected off different surfaces	**Reverberate**
✠ Beat or whip (someone) severely	**Flog**
✠ Beautiful woman; the most beautiful woman in a particular place	**Belle**
✠ Beginning or first appearance of something	**Dawning**
✠ Beginning or origin of something	**Genesis**
✠ Beginning to develop or exist	**Incipient**
✠ Beginning to exist; recently formed or developed	**Nascent**

- ✠ Behaviour that is accepted as socially or morally correct and proper — **Propriety**
- ✠ Behaviour that shows low morals and a great love of pleasure, money, fame, etc — **Decadence**
- ✠ Behaviour in which somebody pretends to have moral standards or opinions that he/she does not actually have — **Hypocrisy**
- ✠ Behaviour, in particular sexual or legally dubious behaviour; considered improper but not seriously so — **Hanky-panky**
- ✠ Beliefs or ideas that are very important to a group — **Tenet**
- ✠ Beliefs or opinions that do not agree with the official belief or opinion of a particular religion — **Heresy**
- ✠ Beliefs that particular events happen in a way that cannot be explained by reason or science — **Superstition**
- ✠ Belonging or relating to heaven — **Celestial**
- ✠ Belonging to a foreign country, supposedly from another world; unfamiliar and disturbing or distasteful — **Alien**
- ✠ Belonging to a particular place rather than coming to it from somewhere else — **Indigenous**
- ✠ Belonging to the basic nature of someone or something — **Inherent**
- ✠ Belonging to the middle class — **Bourgeois**
- ✠ Below or beneath (something) — **Underneath**
- ✠ Bending down or over; doing something that is not honest, fair, etc — **Stoop**
- ✠ Benefits which one enjoys or is entitled to on account of one's job or position — **Perquisite**
- ✠ Best or most important part of something; the point of greatest success or achievement — **Pinnacle**
- ✠ Best or most important person or thing — **Numero uno**
- ✠ Best or most important thing owned or produced by a particular organisation — **Flagship**

✠ Better than all others	**Par excellence**
✠ Blaming or insulting (someone) in strong or violent language	**Vituperate**
✠ Block of stone or wood that is used as the base for a pillar, statue, etc	**Plinth**
✠ Body of remedial substances used in the practice of medicine	**Materia medica**
✠ Books, articles, etc, that discuss a subject carefully and thoroughly	**Treatise**
✠ Border or line that separates two things, such as types of work, groups of people or areas of land	**Demarcation**
✠ Boring or unpleasant work that does not require special skill and usually does not pay much money	**Menial**
✠ Bottom edge of a dress, skirt, or coat	**Hemline**
✠ Break off (a meeting, legal case , or game) with the intention of resuming it later	**Adjourn**
✠ Brief and direct in a way that may seem rude or unfriendly	**Terse**
✠ Brief and usually unplanned fight during a war	**Skirmish**
✠ Brief time when an action or activity stops	**Lull**
✠ Brief trips taken for pleasure	**Jaunt**
✠ Brief trips that people take for fun usually as a group	**Outing**
✠ Brief written messages or reports from one person or department in a company or organisation to another	**Memorandum**
✠ Bringing (someone who is unconscious, not breathing, or close to death) back to a conscious or active state again	**Resuscitate**
✠ Broken parts of a vehicle, building, etc, that has been badly damaged or destroyed	**Wreckage**
✠ Brother or sister	**Sibling**

✠ Building and the area of land that it is on; statement or idea that is accepted as being true and that is used as the basis of an argument	**Premise**
✠ Building in which grain is stored	**Granary**
✠ Building in which the bodies of dead people are burned	**Crematorium**
✠ Building or chamber above or below the ground in which a dead body is kept	**Tomb**
✠ Building or room in which images of stars, planets, etc, are shown on a high, curved ceiling	**Planetarium**
✠ Building that is used for Jewish religious services	**Synagogue**
✠ Building where aircrafts are kept	**Hangar**
✠ Business of making fashionable and expensive clothes for women	**Haute couture**
✠ Businesses that make money through illegal activities; loud, unpleasant noise	**Racket**
✠ By or for each person	**Per capita**

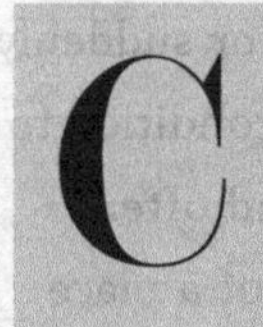

- ✠ Caption to a photograph or other illustration **Cutline**
- ✠ Card from the pack that has been chosen as the most valuable for a particular card game **Trump**
- ✠ Care or maintenance of buildings, equipment, etc **Upkeep**
- ✠ Careful and persistent works or efforts **Diligence**
- ✠ Careful plans or methods for achieving a particular goal usually over a long period of time **Strategy**
- ✠ Cause (a material) to be filled or soaked with something **Impregnate**
- ✠ Cause (someone or something) to receive or take in a large amount of things at the same time **Inundate**
- ✠ Cause (someone) to fall down or be turned over **Upend**
- ✠ Cause (things or people) to separate and go in different directions **Scatter**
- ✠ Cause of pain or harm **Affliction**
- ✠ Centre of public attention **Limelight**
- ✠ Ceremony held for a dead person **Funeral**
- ✠ Ceremony held in a university or college when students receive their degrees **Convocation**
- ✠ Ceremony in which a crown is placed on the head of a new king or queen **Coronation**
- ✠ Certain to die **Mortal**
- ✠ Certain to work properly or succeed **Infallible**
- ✠ Changing (something good) so that it is no longer what it was or should be **Pervert**
- ✠ Changing (something) slightly in order to improve it; to make small adjustments to (something) **Tweak**
- ✠ Changing an earlier statement, opinion or promise because of pressure from somebody/something **Backtrack**

- ✠ Changing direction quickly or suddenly — **Veer**
- ✠ Changing from one state or condition to another — **Transition**
- ✠ Changing moods quickly and often — **Mercurial**
- ✠ Character and atmosphere of a place — **Ambience**
- ✠ Charging an important public figure with a serious crime — **Impeach**
- ✠ Cheerful friendliness; geniality — **Bonhomie**
- ✠ Chemical processes that occur within a living organism in order to maintain life — **Metabolism**
- ✠ Claim or a piece of evidence that one was elsewhere when an act, typically a criminal one , is alleged to have taken place; excuse or pretext — **Alibi**
- ✠ Clear message or request for people to do something — **Clarion call**
- ✠ Clever trick or plan that is used to get someone to do something or to gain an advantage over someone — **Ploy**
- ✠ Climb or moving with difficulty or a lot of effort, using one's hands and feet — **Clamber**
- ✠ Close friend one has worked with, been in the military with, etc — **Comrade**
- ✠ Close relationship with someone or something — **Communion**
- ✠ Close-knit group of interrelated families, large family, or a group of people who are connected because of a particular thing — **Clan**
- ✠ Clothes, especially fine or formal ones — **Attire**
- ✠ Collecting or forming into a mass or group — **Agglomerate**
- ✠ Collectable object such as a piece of furniture or work of art that has a high value because of its age and quality — **Antique**
- ✠ Collection of different things — **Potpourri**
- ✠ Collection of historical documents or records providing information about a place, institution, or group of people — **Archive**

- ✠ Collection of things (such as photographs, stories, facts, etc) that have been gathered together and presented as a group especially in the form of a book **Compendium**
- ✠ Collection of things, which may be similar or different **Collage**
- ✠ Collection of weapons and military equipment **Arsenal**
- ✠ Collection of written or spoken texts **Corpus**
- ✠ Combination of events, state of affairs **Conjuncture**
- ✠ Come at a later time; to happen as a result **Ensue**
- ✠ Comparing between one thing and another, typically for the purpose of explanation or clarification **Analogy**
- ✠ Compelling attractiveness or charm that can inspire devotion in others **Charisma**
- ✠ Competition for young women in which their beauty, personal qualities and skills are judged **Pageant**
- ✠ Complete change of attitude or opinion **Volte-face**
- ✠ Complete control of the entire supply of goods or of a service in a certain area or market **Monopoly**
- ✠ Complete freedom to act as one wishes **Carte blanche**
- ✠ Complete lists of items, typically one in alphabetical or other systematic order **Catalogue**
- ✠ Complete range of different opinions, people, etc **Spectrum**
- ✠ Completely unwilling to change **Intransigent**
- ✠ Complex disputes or arguments **Imbroglio**
- ✠ Complicated and confusing system of connected passage **Maze**
- ✠ Complicated or unpleasant situation that is difficult to get out of or to move through **Morass**
- ✠ Comprising or relating to all sorts or varieties **Omnifarious**
- ✠ Conceal the nature or existence of (a feeling or situation) **Disguise**

✠ Concentrated artillery bombardment over a wide area; large number of something, such as questions or comments, that are directed at somebody very quickly, one after the other, often in an aggressive way	**Barrage**
✠ Conclusion or opinions that are formed because of known facts or evidence	**Inference**
✠ Condition in which a part of one's body becomes red, swollen and painful	**Inflammation**
✠ Condition in which someone is not able to think normally because of being drunk, drugged, tired, etc	**Stupor**
✠ Confused struggles or fights involving many people	**Melee**
✠ Confusing or difficult problem	**Conundrum**
✠ Confusing or meaningless words or activities	**Mumbo-jumbo**
✠ Connected with particular circumstances	**Circumstantial**
✠ Connected with young people who are not yet adults	**Juvenile**
✠ Consequences or after-effects of a significant and unpleasant event	**Aftermath**
✠ Consisting of or using both letters and numerals	**Alphanumeric**
✠ Consisting of things or people that are all the same or all of the same type	**Homogeneous**
✠ Contests, disputes, competitions, etc, in which neither side can gain an advantage or win	**Stalemate**
✠ Continual increase in the price of goods and services	**Inflation**
✠ Continuing without stopping	**Incessant**
✠ Continuous rattling sound as of hard objects falling or striking each other	**Clatter**
✠ Control or affect (something, such as a game or election) in a dishonest way in order to get a desired result	**Rig**
✠ Controlling or influencing a situation in a skilful but sometimes dishonest way	**Manoeuvre**

- ✠ Controlled breeding and rearing of fish **Pisciculture**
- ✠ Conversations in which clever statements and replies are made quickly **Repartee**
- ✠ Correcting something that is unfair or wrong **Redress**
- ✠ Corrupt behaviour in a position of trust, especially in public office **Malversation**
- ✠ Courage or bravery **Valour**
- ✠ Course of action leading nowhere **Blind alley**
- ✠ Courtesy and considerate behaviour towards others **Comity**
- ✠ Covered passages with arches along one or both sides **Arcade**
- ✠ Covered with decorations **Ornate**
- ✠ Created or done for a particular purpose as necessary **Ad hoc**
- ✠ Crime of getting money from someone by the use of force or threats **Extortion**
- ✠ Crime of trying to overthrow one's country's government or of helping one's country's enemies during war **Treason**
- ✠ Crimes or other morally wrong acts ; illegal or immoral behaviour especially by young people **Delinquency**
- ✠ Cruel and unfair treatment by people with power over others **Tyranny**
- ✠ Cry very loudly and noisily **Squall**
- ✠ Curved paths along which something (such as a rocket) moves through the air or through space **Trajectory**
- ✠ Curved paths followed by a planet or an object as it moves around another planet, star, moon, etc **Orbit**
- ✠ Customs or a way of acting or doing things that is widely accepted and followed **Convention**
- ✠ Customers of a shop, bar, or place of entertainment **Clientele**
- ✠ Cut made in something **Incision**

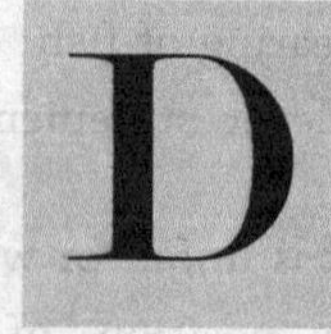

✠ Dance or musical performance **Recital**

✠ Dangers or problems that are hidden or not obvious at first **Pitfall**

✠ Dark and dirty, not fresh or clean **Dingy**

✠ Dark and underground prisons in castles **Dungeon**

✠ Date or time when something must be finished, the last day, hour, or minute on that something will be accepted **Deadline**

✠ Days when day and night are of the same length **Equinox**

✠ Dead bodies of animals **Carcass**

✠ Dead persons who leave the grave at night to bite and suck the blood of living people **Vampire**

✠ Decayed mixture of plants (such as leaves and grass) that is used to improve the soil in a garden **Compost**

✠ Decayed with usually a very bad or disgusting smell **Putrid**

✠ Deceiving or to trick (someone), to persuade (someone) by telling lies **Con(v)**

✠ Deep unconscious state, usually lasting a long time and caused by serious illness or injury **Coma**

✠ Deep, wet sand into which heavy objects sink easily **Quicksand**

✠ Deeply religious, devoted to a particular religion **Devout**

✠ Defeating (someone or something) easily and thoroughly **Trounce**

✠ Defeating (someone) easily and completely in a game or contest **Rout**

✠ Defeating and gaining control of (someone or something) by the use of force	**Subjugate**
✠ Defeating or tricking (someone) by being more intelligent or clever	**Outsmart**
✠ Delay doing something until a later time because one does not want to do it, because one is lazy	**Procrastinate**
✠ Describing (someone or something) as unimportant, weak, bad, etc	**Disparage**
✠ Designed or intended to teach people something	**Didactic**
✠ Desire to cause harm to another person	**Malice**
✠ Determined not to change one's opinion or attitude; difficult to deal with, remove, etc	**Stubborn**
✠ Developing friendlier relations between countries or groups of people who have been enemies	**Rapprochement**
✠ Dictionary of the special terms in a particular field or job	**Glossary**
✠ Die because one is unable to breathe	**Suffocate**
✠ Difference between two opposite things; a division into two opposite groups	**Dichotomy**
✠ Difference especially between things that should be the same	**Discrepancy**
✠ Difficult and unpleasant to do or deal with	**Onerous**
✠ Difficult to handle, control, or deal with because of being large, heavy, or complex	**Unwieldy**
✠ Difficult to understand, having or seeming to have a hidden meaning	**Cryptic**
✠ Direct descent from an ancestor; ancestry or pedigree	**Lineage**
✠ Disappointing end to an exciting or impressive series of events	**Anticlimax**
✠ Disease or disorder that involves a particular group of signs and symptoms	**Syndrome**
✠ Disease that spreads over a whole country or the whole world	**Pandemic**

- ✠ Disguising of military personnel, equipment, and installations by painting or covering them to make them blend in with their surrounding **Camouflage**
- ✠ Dishonest or immoral persons **Sleaze**
- ✠ Displaying wealth, knowledge, etc, in a way that is meant to attract attention, admiration, or envy **Ostentatious**
- ✠ Distance of a place east or west of the Greenwich meridian, measured in degrees **Longitude**
- ✠ Distance of a place north or south of the equator (the line around the world dividing north and south), measured in degrees **Latitude**
- ✠ Doing activities for fun or enjoyment **Play-off**
- ✠ Doing better than (someone or something) ; to be more successful than (someone or something) **Outdo**
- ✠ Doing something that is not allowed; to disobey a command or law **Transgress**
- ✠ Doctor's opinion about how someone will recover from an illness or injury **Prognosis**
- ✠ Done or given because one wants to and not because one is forced to **Voluntary**
- ✠ Dramatic works in which all or most of the words are sung to music; works of this type as an art form or entertainment **Opera**
- ✠ Drawing or pictures that show only the shape of an object **Outline**
- ✠ Dull and ordinary **Mundane**
- ✠ Dull or socially inept person, especially someone who is excessively studious **Spod**

- ✠ Eager to own and collect things — **Acquisitive**
- ✠ Easily affected, influenced, or harmed by something — **Susceptible**
- ✠ Easily annoyed or angered and likely to argue — **Truculent**
- ✠ Easily hurt or harmed physically, mentally, or emotionally; open to attack, harm, or damage — **Vulnerable**
- ✠ Easily managed or controlled; willing to learn or be guided by another — **Tractable**
- ✠ Eating both plants and animals; eager to learn about many different things — **Omnivorous**
- ✠ Economic situations where there is high inflation (prices rising continuously) but no increase in the jobs that are available or in business activity — **Stagflation**
- ✠ Effective from a particular date in the past — **Retrospective**
- ✠ Elaborate or glib speeches or stories, typically those used by a salesperson — **Spiel**
- ✠ E-mails that are not wanted ; an e-mail that is sent to large numbers of people and that consists mostly of advertising — **Spam**
- ✠ Embarrassing social mistake — **Faux pas**
- ✠ Ending a romantic relationship with (someone) in a sudden and painful way — **Jilt**
- ✠ Ending an organisation or group (such as a club) — **Disband**
- ✠ End or failure of an institution, an idea, a company, etc; death of a person — **Demise**
- ✠ Enjoy (something) for a long time — **Savour**
- ✠ Enjoying oneself or celebrating in a noisy or boisterous way — **Roister**

✠ Enjoyable in a lively or noisy way	**Rollicking**
✠ Enjoyments that someone gets from being violent or cruel or from causing pain	**Sadism**
✠ Entering (someone) as a member of or being a participant in something	**Enroll**
✠ Entering or appearing somewhere suddenly and with a lot of force	**Irrupt**
✠ Enthusiastic and vocal supporters of someone or something	**Cheerleader**
✠ Enthusiastic clapping by an audience as a sign of their approval	**Ovation**
✠ Error in the way a law, rule, or contract is written that makes it possible for some people to legally avoid obeying it	**Loophole**
✠ Events causing great and usually sudden damage or suffering; a disaster	**Catastrophe**
✠ Events involving destruction or damage on a catastrophic scale	**Apocalypse**
✠ Events marked by festivities or celebration	**Fiesta**
✠ Event or a short period of time that is important or unusual	**Episode**
✠ Events or situations in which many people are killed and many things are destroyed especially by fire	**Holocaust**
✠ Events that may or may not happen	**Contingency**
✠ Exact or very close copy of something	**Replica**
✠ Examinations intended to qualify successful candidates for higher education	**Baccalaureate**
✠ Examples that represent or express something very well	**Epitome**
✠ Excessive emotional or psychological reliance on a partner	**Codependency**
✠ Exchanging goods, property, services, etc for other goods, etc without using money	**Barter**

✠ Excluding (someone) from a group	**Ostracize**
✠ Existing as a basic part of a person's nature or character	**Inbred**
✠ Existing from the beginning of time ; very ancient	**Primordial**
✠ Existing or continuing in the same way for a long time	**Perennial**
✠ Existing or happening in the same time period	**Contemporary**
✠ Existing, but not yet very noticeable, active or well developed	**Latent**
✠ Experiences that are very unpleasant or difficult	**Ordeal**
✠ Experienced or felt by watching, hearing about, or reading about someone else rather than by doing something yourself	**Vicarious**
✠ Expressing doubts about whether something is right, honest, etc	**Impugn**
✠ Expressing severe disapprovals of (someone or something), especially in a formal statement	**Censure**
✠ Expressing feelings or opinions in a very loud or forceful way	**Vociferous**
✠ Expressing opinions or criticism in a very forceful and often annoying or unpleasant way	**Strident**
✠ Expressions designed to call something to mind without mentioning it explicitly; an indirect or passing reference	**Allusion**
✠ Expressions of strong anger or disapproval by many people	**Outcry**
✠ Extensive groups of islands	**Archipelago**
✠ Extra vote given by a chairperson to decide an issue when the votes on each side are equal	**Casting vote**
✠ Extracting money from (someone) by fine or taxation	**Mulct**
✠ Extreme anger ; a strong feeling of unhappiness because of something bad, hurtful, or morally wrong	**Outrage**

- ✠ Extreme physical or mental sufferings **Agony**
- ✠ Extreme self-confidence or audacity (usually used approvingly) **Chutzpah**
- ✠ Extremely easy tasks **Cinch**
- ✠ Extremely excited and enthusiastic about doing something **Gung ho**
- ✠ Extremely good and deserving to be admired and copied **Exemplary**
- ✠ Extremely or unusually small **Diminutive**
- ✠ Extremely strong dislikes or fears of someone or something **Phobia**

- ✠ Facts or the process of ending or being brought to an end **Cessation**
- ✠ Failing to show proper respect and courtesy **Impudent**
- ✠ Failure to fulfil an obligation ; something that happens or is done when nothing else has been done or can be done **Default**
- ✠ Familiar or humorous names given to a person or thing instead of the real name **Nickname**
- ✠ Families of rulers who rule over a country for a long period of time **Dynasty**
- ✠ Famous persons, especially in entertainment or sports **Celebrity**
- ✠ Farmers in the past who owned a small amount of land ; very good, hard, and valuable work that someone does especially to support a cause, to help a team, etc **Yeoman**
- ✠ Features (such as mountains and rivers) in an area of land **Topography**
- ✠ Feeling a strong desire or wish for something or to do something **Yearn**
- ✠ Feeling nervous because the ending is not known until the final moment **Nail-biting**
- ✠ Feeling or showing great sadness because someone has died **Mourn**
- ✠ Feeling sorrow or regreting for (something) **Rue**
- ✠ Feeling of being sorry for doing something bad or wrong in the past **Remorse**

✠ Feelings of deep anxiety or dread, typically an unfocused one about the human condition or the state of the world in general	**Angst**
✠ Feelings of doubt or uncertainty about whether one is doing the right thing	**Qualm**
✠ Feelings of enjoyment and enthusiasm	**Zest**
✠ Feelings of foolish or very strong love or admiration for someone or something	**Infatuation**
✠ Feelings of great happiness and excitement	**Euphoria**
✠ Feelings of guilt or regret	**Compunction**
✠ Feelings of like or dislike for someone or something especially when it is not reasonable or logical	**Prejudice**
✠ Feelings of sadness mixed with pleasure and affection when one thinks of happy times in the past	**Nostalgia**
✠ Feelings of strong dislike or disapproval of someone or something you think does not deserve respect	**Disdain**
✠ Feelings or beliefs that bad things will happen in the future	**Pessimism**
✠ Feelings or beliefs that good things will happen in the future	**Optimism**
✠ Feelings or expressing overwhelming happiness or joyful excitement	**Ecstatic**
✠ Feelings or a particular quality that is very noticeable and seems to surround a person or place	**Aura**
✠ Feelings or showing a lack of courage or confidence	**Timid**
✠ Feelings that someone or something gives you	**Vibe**
✠ Feelings that one has already experienced something that is actually happening for the first time; something that has happened many times before something that is very familiar	**Déjà vu**

✠ Female ballet dancers	**Danseuse**
✠ Fictitious or factual works describing a series of events	**Chronicle**
✠ Fights between women	**Catfight**
✠ Fights, briefly and usually not very seriously	**Scuffle**
✠ Figures shaped like a human body that is used for making or displaying clothes	**Mannequin**
✠ Filled with or showing sexual desire	**Lascivious**
✠ First time an actor, musician, athlete, etc, does something in public or for the public	**Debut**
✠ Fixed sum of money paid to someone each year, typically for the rest of their life	**Annuity**
✠ Flat cases for carrying documents or drawings, investments that are owned by a person or organisation	**Portfolio**
✠ Fleet of warships	**Armada**
✠ Flowing out of something in a fast and forceful way	**Spew**
✠ Following, watching, and bothering (someone) constantly in a way that is frightening, dangerous, etc	**Stalk**
✠ Food that a person or animal usually eats	**Diet**
✠ Food that is cooked in a particular way, style of cooking	**Cuisine**
✠ Foolish talks or ideas	**Guff**
✠ Foolish, confused, or meaningless words	**Gibberish**
✠ For an intervening or temporary period of time	**Ad interim**
✠ Forcing someone to go somewhere with you, often using threats or violence	**Abduction**
✠ Forceful or angry speeches	**Harangue**
✠ Forming an opinion about something without definitely knowing the truth	**Surmise**
✠ Form of punishments or tortures that involved caning the soles of someone's feet	**Bastinado**

- ✠ Formal acts or the process of placing someone into a new job, position, government office **Induction**
- ✠ Formal ceremonies or series of acts that are always performed in the same way **Ritual**
- ✠ Formal meetings in which representatives or experts discuss important matters, make decisions, etc **Congress**
- ✠ Formal processions of people walking, on horseback, or riding in vehicles **Cavalcade**
- ✠ Formally choosing someone as a candidate for a job, position, office, etc **Nominate**
- ✠ Formations of clear and distinct sounds in speech **Articulation**
- ✠ Fortresses, typically one on high ground above a city **Citadel**
- ✠ Formal and serious promises to tell the truth or to do something **Oath**
- ✠ Fraudulent or dishonest acts or practices **Rort**
- ✠ Fraudulent practices of sending emails purporting to be from reputable companies in order to induce individuals to reveal personal information **Phishing**
- ✠ Freedom from being required to do something that others are required to do **Exemption**
- ✠ Freedom from punishment, harm, or loss **Impunity**
- ✠ Freedom to do something the way you want to do it **Leeway**
- ✠ Friendly relationships **Rapport**
- ✠ Friendly remarks and jokes **Banter**
- ✠ Full and wide view of something **Panorama**
- ✠ Full of anger, arguments and bad feelings **Acrimonious**
- ✠ Full of clever tricks : very clever **Wily**
- ✠ Full of hate or anger, extremely or excessively harsh or strong **Virulent**
- ✠ Funny and clever **Witty**
- ✠ Funny plays or movies about ridiculous situations and events **Farce**

✠ General laws, rules, principles, or criteria by which something is judged	**Canon**
✠ General or basic quality or meaning of something	**Tenor**
✠ Generous and friendly treatment of visitors and guests	**Hospitality**
✠ Genuine, real or legal; not false	**Bona fide**
✠ Girlfriends of criminals	**Moll**
✠ Giving a brief summary of something	**Recapitulate**
✠ Giving or being a sign of (something that will happen or develop in the future)	**Presage**
✠ Giving somebody a signal using your finger or hand, especially to tell them to move nearer or to follow you	**Beckon**
✠ Giving up (something) ; to give (something, such as power, control, or possession) to another person or group	**Relinquish**
✠ Giving help or support to the main group of workers	**Auxiliary**
✠ Going in a direction that is away from a group or from the place where one should be	**Stray**
✠ Going on someone's land without permission	**Trespass**
✠ Goods that are bought and sold	**Merchandise**
✠ Government departments that control public money	**Exchequer**
✠ Governments formed by two or more political parties working together	**Coalition**
✠ Government official who is the representative of his or her country in a foreign country	**Consul**

✠ Government orders that limit trade in some way	**Embargo**
✠ Gradual increase in noise ; the loudest point of a period of continuous noise	**Crescendo**
✠ Gradual reduction in the size of a business, activity, etc	**Runown**
✠ Great and often wild or uncontrolled activities	**Frenzy**
✠ Great disaster or complete failure	**Debacle**
✠ Great number of things or people	**Multitude**
✠ Great technical skill and brilliance shown in a performance or activity	**Bravura**
✠ Great work ; the greatest achievement of an artist or a writer	**Magnum opus**
✠ Groups of animals or plants that are similar and can produce young animals or plants	**Species**
✠ Groups of members of the public who listen to the facts of a case in a court and decide whether or not somebody is guilty of a crime	**Jury**
✠ Groups of military ships commanded by the same person	**Fleet**
✠ Groups of musicians who play usually classical music together and who are led by a conductor	**Orchestra**
✠ Groups of officials led by an ambassador who represent their government in a foreign country ; building in which an embassy works	**Embassy**
✠ Groups of people or businesses that work together	**Syndicate**
✠ Groups of people who are doing something together	**Platoon**
✠ Groups of people who are the leaders of an action or movement in society, politics, art, etc	**Vanguard**
✠ Groups of people who are together for a particular purpose	**Posse**
✠ Groups of people who go with and assist an important person	**Entourage**

- ✠ Groups of people who have gathered to watch or listen to something (a play, concert, somebody speaking, etc) **Audience**
- ✠ Groups of people who have the same job, interests, etc **Fraternity**
- ✠ Groups of people who operate a ship, airplane, or train **Crew**
- ✠ Groups of people who share a common feature or aspect of behaviour **Cohort**
- ✠ Groups of people with shared concerns within a political party or larger organisation **Caucus**
- ✠ Groups of people, companies, etc, that agree to work together **Consortium**
- ✠ Groups of people, countries, organisations, etc, that are joined together in some activity or effort **Confederation**
- ✠ Groups of people, especially traders or pilgrims, travelling together across a desert in Asia or North Africa **Caravan**
- ✠ Groups of separate companies that agree to increase profits by fixing prices and not competing with each other **Cartel**
- ✠ Groups of singers or dancers performing together in a supporting role in a musical or opera **Chorus**
- ✠ Groups of vehicles or ships that are travelling together usually for protection **Convoy**
- ✠ Groups or organisation of nations or people united for a purpose **League**
- ✠ Groups within a larger group that have different ideas and opinions than the rest of the group **Faction**
- ✠ Guiding beliefs of a person, group, or organisation **Ethos**

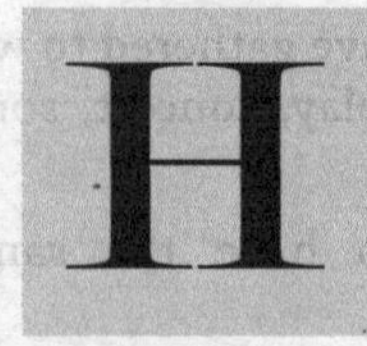

✠ Happening after death, medical examination of the body of a dead person to determine the cause of death	**Post-mortem**
✠ Happening as a result of something	**Consequent**
✠ Happening at the same time	**Concurrent**
✠ Happening often but not regularly ; not constant or steady	**Sporadic**
✠ Happening or appearing again and again	**Recurrent**
✠ Happening or appearing in many places and not unusual ; very common or ordinary	**Common place**
✠ Happening or popular at a particular time	**Du jour**
✠ Happening, done, or published after someone's death	**Posthumous**
✠ Happy and enjoyable scenes or experience	**Idyll**
✠ Happy and lively in a way that is attractive	**Vivacious**
✠ Harming (someone) through sexual contact ; to touch (someone) in a sexual and improper way	**Molest**
✠ Harsh and angry words	**Vitriolic**
✠ Harsh criticisms that show a lack of respect or approval for someone or something	**Scorn**
✠ Harsh discordant mixture of sounds	**Cacophony**
✠ Harsh or critical statements about someone	**Obloquy**
✠ Having (something) as a part, step, or result	**Entail**
✠ Having a speech problem that causes one to repeat the beginning sound of some words	**Stutter**
✠ Having a dull or uninteresting appearance ; not attractive or stylish	**Dowdy**

- ✠ Having a good or helpful result especially after something unpleasant has happened — **Salutary**
- ✠ Having a pleasant, spicy taste ; interesting and exciting — **Piquant**
- ✠ Having a strong and unpleasant smell or taste from no longer being fresh — **Rancid**
- ✠ Having a strong, sharp taste or smell — **Pungent**
- ✠ Having a very appealing taste or smell — **Luscious**
- ✠ Having a very noticeable quality that attracts a lot of attention — **Flamboyant**
- ✠ Having an obstinately uncooperative attitude towards authority or discipline — **Recalcitrant**
- ✠ Having complete or unlimited power — **Omnipotent**
- ✠ Having fair hair and a light complexion — **Blonde**
- ✠ Having many twists and turns; complicated, long, and confusing — **Tortuous**
- ✠ Having mixed feelings or contradictory ideas about something or someone — **Ambivalent**
- ✠ Having no legal power — **Null**
- ✠ Having no useful purpose — **Otiose**
- ✠ Having or relating to two sides ; affecting both sides, involving two parties, especially countries — **Bilateral**
- ✠ Having or showing a desire to hurt someone who has hurt or caused problems for you — **Vindictive**
- ✠ Having or showing a lot of courage or determination — **Plucky**
- ✠ Having or showing a lot of violence and blood — **Gory**
- ✠ Having or showing an ability to understand difficult ideas and situations and to make good decisions — **Sagacious**
- ✠ Having or showing courage, be very brave or courageous — **Valiant**

✠ Having or showing knowledge that is learned by studying	**Erudite**
✠ Having people of different types or from different countries, and influenced by their culture, showing an interest in different cultures, ideas	**Cosmopolitan**
✠ Having the qualities or appearance considered to be typical of men	**Masculine**
✠ Having very fixed beliefs and being unlikely or unwilling to change them	**Hardliner**
✠ Heavy automatic guns that fire shells from an aircraft or tank	**Cannon**
✠ Height of an object or point in relation to sea level or ground level	**Altitude**
✠ Helping someone or something pay for the costs of (something)	**Subsidise**
✠ Highest point in the development of something ; a climax or culmination	**Apogee**
✠ Highest point of a mountain, the top of a mountain	**Summit**
✠ History of the family members in a person's or animal's past especially when it is good or impressive	**Pedigree**
✠ Hitting (someone or something) very hard with a stick, whip, etc	**Thrash**
✠ Hitting (someone) on the buttocks with one's hand as a form of punishment	**Spank**
✠ Hitting or beating something or someone and make a loud, deep sound	**Thump**
✠ Hitting something with a loud, dull sound	**Thud**
✠ Honour or fame given for some achievement	**Laurel**
✠ Honour or respect that is felt for or shown to (someone or something)	**Reverence**
✠ Hopeful or romantic in a way that is not practical	**Quixotic**

✠ Houses or part of a house in which the women of a Muslim household live	**Harem**
✠ Houses where men visit prostitutes	**Brothel**
✠ Humour that shows the weaknesses or bad qualities of a person, government, society, etc	**Satire**
✠ Humorous in a clever and often ironic way	**Wry**
✠ Humorous rhyming poem of five lines	**Limerick**
✠ Hundredth anniversary of a significant event	**Centenary**

- Ideas about doing something that is far removed from normal reality — **Fantasy**
- Ideas or beliefs that people are born again with a different body after death — **Reincarnation**
- Ideas or inventions which are considered to be a particular person's creation — **Brainchild**
- Ideas or sets of beliefs that guide the actions of a person or group — **Credo**
- Idea or a set of principles or religious beliefs — **Creed**
- Idea or theory that are not proven but that lead to further study or discussion — **Hypothesis**
- Ideas suggested by a word in addition to its main meaning — **Connotation**
- Ideas or statements that are often false or exaggerated and that are spread in order to help a cause, a political leader, a government, etc — **Propaganda**
- Ideas or stories that are not true but that many people have heard or read — **Folklore**
- Illness persisting for a long time or constantly recurring — **Chronic**
- Imaginary places in which the government, laws, and social conditions are perfect — **Utopia**
- Imaginary sea creatures that have a woman's head and body and a fish's tail instead of legs — **Mermaid**
- Impartial advisers to a court of law in a particular case — **Amicus curiae**
- Important, real, or meaningful — **Substantive**
- Impossible to defeat or discourage — **Indomitable**

✠ Impossible to defeat or overcome	**Invincible**
✠ Impossible to harm, damage, or defeat	**Invulnerable**
✠ Impossible to solve or get control of ; impossible to overcome	**Insurmountable**
✠ Impressive display or range of a particular type of thing	**Array**
✠ In a careless and unplanned way	**Willy-nilly**
✠ In a confused and careless way	**Helter-skelter**
✠ In a state of tremulous excitement	**Aflutter**
✠ In a very bad condition and needing to be repaired	**Ramshackle**
✠ In an uncertain or undecided state or condition	**Limbo**
✠ In great disorder or confusion	**Topsy-turvy**
✠ In preparation or progress; happening or beginning to happen	**Afoot**
✠ In a very bad condition because of age or lack of care	**Dilapidated**
✠ Including many different things ; full of variety	**Variegated**
✠ Increased effectiveness that results when two or more people or businesses work together	**Synergy**
✠ Indefinite and very long period of time	**Aeon**
✠ Independent persons or a body officially appointed to settle a dispute	**Arbitrator**
✠ Indirect and usually bad results of an action or event that may happen some time afterwards	**Repercussion**
✠ Influence or control over another country, a group of people	**Hegemony**
✠ Influence or power, especially in politics or business	**Clout**
✠ Informal ways of spreading information or rumors through conversation	**Grapevine**
✠ Information about a person and about what they have done in their life	**Biodata**

✠ Inscriptions on a building, statue, or coin	**Epigraph**
✠ Institutions, places, or persons strongly maintaining particular principles, attitudes, or activities	**Bastion**
✠ Insulting remarks made in public	**Brickbats**
✠ Intense military campaign intended to bring about a swift victory	**Blitzkrieg**
✠ Introduction to a book or speech	**Preface**
✠ Introduction to a book, play, etc	**Prologue**
✠ Involving a chance that something bad or unpleasant could happen	**Dicey**
✠ Involving a lot of violence, confusion, or disorder	**Tumultuous**
✠ Involving death or violence in a way that is strange, frightening, or unpleasant	**Macabre**
✠ Involving only one group or country	**Unilateral**
✠ Items of additional material added at the end of a book or other publication	**Addendum**

✠ Japanese art of folding paper into shapes that look like birds, animals, etc	**Origami**
✠ Japanese flower arranging, that has strict formal rules	**Ikebana**
✠ Japanese form of self-defence and martial art that uses locks, holds, throws, and the opponent's own movements	**Aikido**
✠ Jargon or slang of a particular group or class	**Argot**
✠ Jobs, activities, etc, that are very suitable for someone	**Niche**
✠ Journal or newspaper, especially the official one of an organisation or institution	**Gazette**
✠ Journalist who is not on the regular staff of a newspaper but who writes stories for that newspaper	**Stringer**
✠ Journey especially by a group of people for a specific purpose	**Expedition**

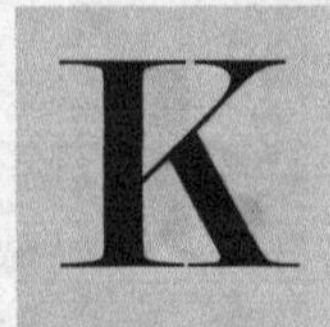

- ✠ Killing (a person or animal) by squeezing the throat **Strangle**
- ✠ Killing (an animal) for food, kill (many people) in a very violent way **Slaughter**
- ✠ Killing (someone) illegally as punishment for a crime **Lynch**
- ✠ Killing of a large number of people **Carnage**
- ✠ Killing or wounding of people, typically on a large scale during a conflict **Bloodshed**
- ✠ Kindness shown to somebody when he/she is being punished; willingness not to punish somebody so severely **Clemency**
- ✠ Knowing everything; having unlimited understanding or knowledge **Omniscient**
- ✠ Knowing or using several languages **Polyglot**

- ✠ Lack of agreements between people, ideas, etc **Discord**
- ✠ Lack of order; a confused or messy condition **Disarray**
- ✠ Lack of respect or dislike for someone or something **Contempt**
- ✠ Lack of seriousness **Levity**
- ✠ Lack of solidity or substance; thinness **Tenuity**
- ✠ Lack of the usual social or ethical standards in an individual or group **Anomie (anomy)**
- ✠ Lacking confidence; not feeling comfortable around people, very careful about acting or speaking **Diffident**
- ✠ Land used or suitable for growing crops **Arable**
- ✠ Language used in conversation but not in formal speech or writing **Colloquial**
- ✠ Legislative body having two chambers **Bicameral**
- ✠ Language of ordinary speeches rather than formal writing **Vernacular**
- ✠ Language or behaviour that is nonsense and is intended to hide the truth from people **Hocus-pocus**
- ✠ Language that is intended to influence people and that may not be honest or reasonable **Rhetoric**
- ✠ Language that is used among people who speak various different languages **Lingua franca**
- ✠ Language used by a particular group of people **Parlance**
- ✠ Language used for a particular activity or by a particular group of people **Jargon**

✠ Large amount of money that has been given to a school, hospital, etc, and that is used to pay for its creation and continuing support : person's natural ability or talent	**Endowment**
✠ Large amount of rain that suddenly falls in an area ; large amount of things that come at the same time	**Deluge**
✠ Large amount of something that is released suddenly	**Torrent**
✠ Large and beautiful view of an area of land or water	**Vista**
✠ Large and very unpleasant amount of dirt	**Filth**
✠ Large areas of land that have been farmed too much with the result that plants will not grow there	**Badlands**
✠ Large buildings or group of buildings for soldiers to live in	**Barracks**
✠ Large burial ground, especially one not in a churchyard	**Cemetery**
✠ Large business that is made of different kinds of companies	**Conglomerate**
✠ Large cages, buildings, or enclosures for keeping birds in	**Aviary**
✠ Large group of people or things of a particular kind	**Bevy**
✠ Large group of people, especially an organised group with a particular purpose	**Battalion**
✠ Large group of people	**Throng**
✠ Large notices or signs put up in a public place or carried by people	**Placard**
✠ Large number of things that appear or happen in a short period of time	**Spate**
✠ Large open-air fire used for burning rubbish or as part of a celebration	**Bonfire**

✠ Large parties or celebrations	**Fete**
✠ Large parties or celebrations	**Jamboree**
✠ Large tents used for social or commercial functions ; covered structures over the entrance to a building	**Marquee**
✠ Large-calibre guns used in warfare on land	**Artillery**
✠ Lasting for a very short time	**Evanescent/ Ephemeral**
✠ Late morning meals eaten instead of breakfast and lunch	**Brunch**
✠ Laws or regulations made by a government	**Ordinance**
✠ Laws or rules that limit or control something ; strong criticism	**Stricture**
✠ Leaving (property) to a person or other beneficiary by a will	**Bequeath**
✠ Legal agreements in which a person borrows money to buy property (such as a house) and pays back the money over a period of years	**Mortgage**
✠ Legal right to be the only one to reproduce, publish, and sell a book, musical recording, etc, for a certain period of time	**Copyright**
✠ Letter or group of letters that is added at the beginning of a word to change its meaning	**Prefix**
✠ Level of respect that people have for a successful person, organisation, etc	**Stature**
✠ Light that is placed somewhere to guide vehicles and warn them of danger	**Beacon**
✠ Likely to change in a very sudden or extreme way ; likely to become dangerous or out of control	**Volatile**
✠ Likely to have or produce good results	**Propitious**
✠ Limited to a small number of people	**Esoteric**
✠ Lines in a newspaper naming the writer of an article	**Byline**

- ✠ Lines notionally drawn on the Earth equidistant from the poles **Equator**
- ✠ Lines on a weather map that join places that have the same air pressure at a particular time **Isobar**
- ✠ Lines on a weather map that join places that have the same temperature at a particular time **Isotherm**
- ✠ Lines that have a series of short, sharp turns or angles **Zigzag**
- ✠ Lists of items required, things to be done, or points to be considered, used as a reminder **Checklist**
- ✠ Lists of the books referred to in a scholarly work , typically printed as an appendix **Bibliography**
- ✠ Lists of the foods that may be ordered at a restaurant **Menu**
- ✠ Lists of the people or things that belong to a particular group, team, etc **Roster**
- ✠ Lists of the people who work for a company and the amount of money that the company has agreed to pay them **Payroll**
- ✠ Lists that show who must do a certain job **Rota**
- ✠ Lively or energetic quality **Vitality**
- ✠ Living in trees **Arboreal**
- ✠ Long and angry fights or quarrels between two people or two groups **Feud**
- ✠ Long and angry speechs **Tirade**
- ✠ Long and complicated series of events **Saga**
- ✠ Long and determined efforts to achieve something that one believes to be right or to stop something that one believes to be wrong **Crusade**
- ✠ Long journeys to a distant or unknown place especially over water or through outer space **Voyage**
- ✠ Long poems that tell the story of a hero's adventures **Epic**

✠ Long speeches given by a character in a story, movie, play, etc, or by a performer	**Monologue**
✠ Long, complicated, and annoying process, descriptions	**Rigmarole**
✠ Long, narrow boxes, typically of wood, in which a dead body is buried or cremated	**Coffin**
✠ Long, thin sticks used by a magician or during magic tricks	**Wand**
✠ Long, usually serious speeches that a character in a play make to an audience and that reveal the character's thoughts	**Soliloquy**
✠ Long-term security yielding a fixed rate of interest, issued by a company and secured against assets	**Debenture**
✠ Looking at someone in an evil or unpleasantly sexual way	**Leer**
✠ Looking for private information about someone or something	**Snoop**
✠ Lots of energy and style	**Panache**
✠ Loud and confused noises, strongly expressed protest or demand from a large number of people	**Clamour**
✠ Loud, confusing mixture of noises that lasts for a long time	**Din**
✠ Loving and admiring oneself and especially one's appearance too much	**Narcissism**
✠ Low sound made when many people are speaking	**Murmur**
✠ Low, continuous humming or murmuring sound, made by or similar to that made by an insect ; atmosphere of excitement and activity	**Buzz**
✠ Lowest possible level	**Rock-bottom**
✠ Loyalty or commitment to a superior or to a group or cause	**Allegiance**

- ✠ Made by combining different substances ; not natural **Synthetic**
- ✠ Made or done without preparation **Impromptu**
- ✠ Made to be useful rather than to be decorative or comfortable **Utilitarian**
- ✠ Made to look like an exact copy of something in order to trick people **Counterfeit**
- ✠ Made up of different things **Sundry**
- ✠ Made up of many different people or things **Motley**
- ✠ Made up of parts that are different **Heterogeneous**
- ✠ Magical liquid that can cure illness or extend life **Elixir**
- ✠ Main characters in a novel, play, movie, etc **Protagonist**
- ✠ Main group of people in a Communist government who make decisions about policy **Politburo**
- ✠ Main or central part of a city or town **Downtown**
- ✠ Major changes or a period of change that causes a lot of conflict, confusion, anger, etc **Upheaval**
- ✠ Make an idea, belief, etc known to many people **Promulgate**
- ✠ Making someone or something weaker or less effective usually in a secret or gradual way **Undermine**
- ✠ Making someone feel or look young, healthy, or energetic again **Rejuvenate**
- ✠ Making someone want to know more about something **Intrigue**
- ✠ Making something as good or as effective as possible **Optimise**
- ✠ Making something better or like new again **Revamp**

✠ Making something valid ; to state or show that something is legal	**Validate**
✠ Making something very dry	**Parch**
✠ Make a formal judgement on a disputed matter	**Adjudicate**
✠ Making a low, heavy, continuous sound or series of sounds	**Rumble**
✠ Making a short, high-pitched cry or noise	**Squeak**
✠ Making an amount or supply of something last longer by using or consuming it frugally ; manage to make a living with difficulty	**Eke**
✠ Making something full again by replacing what has been used	**Replenish**
✠ Male former pupil or student of a particular school, college, or university	**Alumnus (pl. alumni)**
✠ Maleness in an aggressive way	**Macho**
✠ Man dressing and acting in an appealing and sophisticated way ; fashionable, attractive, and confident	**Debonair**
✠ Man in ancient Rome who fought against another man or animal for public entertainment	**Gladiator**
✠ Man on his wedding day or just before and after the event	**Bridegroom**
✠ Man who cares a lot about his clothes and appearance	**Dandy**
✠ Man who controls a family, group, or government	**Patriarch**
✠ Man who hates women	**Misogynist**
✠ Man who is an expert at writing, conducting, or teaching music	**Maestro**
✠ Man who is dishonest or immoral	**Rogue**
✠ Man who is paid by a woman to be her lover and companion	**Gigolo**
✠ Man who makes money illegally by getting customers for prostitutes	**Pimp**

- ✠ Man who wants to marry a particular woman **Suitor**
- ✠ Managing or using money in a careful or wise way **Thrifty**
- ✠ Many changes or problems that happen over time **Vicissitude**
- ✠ Mark or quality that shows what something is or what it could be **Earmark**
- ✠ Mark that is left on one's skin after a wound heals ; feeling of great emotional pain or sadness that is caused by a bad experience and that lasts for a long time **Scar**
- ✠ Materials made of a network of wire or thread ; complex or constricting situation **Mesh**
- ✠ Materials that are flowing out **Efflux**
- ✠ Meal consisting of several dishes from which guests serve themselves **Buffet**
- ✠ Meal to which everyone who is invited brings food to share **Pot luck**
- ✠ Measures designed merely to humour or placate someone **Placebo**
- ✠ Member of a group of people who moves from place to place instead of living in one place all the time **Nomad**
- ✠ Member of a religion (such as Christianity, Judaism, and Islam) who delivers messages that are believed to have come from God **Prophet**
- ✠ Mental illness in which a person becomes very emotional or excited **Mania**
- ✠ Mental state in which one is confused and not able to think or speak clearly, a state of wild excitement and great happiness **Delirium**
- ✠ Metal made by combining two or more metallic elements **Alloy**
- ✠ Method of producing coloured designs on textiles by dyeing them **Batik**

✠ Method or trick that is used to get people's attention or to sell something	**Gimmick**
✠ Military group controlling a government after taking control of it by force	**Junta**
✠ Military supplies including weapons, ammunition, armour, vehicles, etc	**Ordnance**
✠ Mistake made because someone forgets or fails to notice something	**Oversight**
✠ Mixture of different things	**Mélange**
✠ Modern soldiers who fight in armoured vehicles	**Cavalry**
✠ Money given as a reward	**Bounty**
✠ Money or food given to poor people	**Alms**
✠ Money or property that is given to you by somebody when he/she dies	**Legacy**
✠ Money that is less than the amount that is needed	**Deficit**
✠ Money that is owed and should have been paid earlier	**Arrears**
✠ Money that is paid in order to free someone who has been captured or kidnapped	**Ransom**
✠ Money that you have to pay by law to your former wife or husband after separation	**Alimony**
✠ Moral fables, especially one with animals as characters	**Apologue**
✠ Morally good behaviour or character	**Virtue**
✠ Most important and basic facts or details about something	**Nitty-gritty**
✠ Most important idea or part of something	**Keynote**
✠ Most important part of something (such as a problem, issue, puzzle, etc)	**Crux**
✠ Most important part of something	**Quintessence**
✠ Most successful or powerful group of people	**Elite**
✠ Moving about quickly from side to side or up and down	**Jiggle**

✠ Moving at a speed faster than walking by stepping with each front leg at the same time as the opposite back leg	**Trot**
✠ Moving or acting quickly to do, find, or get something often before someone else does	**Scramble**
✠ Moving or acting too slowly	**Dawdle**
✠ Move or lift (something) so that it is no longer smooth	**Ruffle**
✠ Moving quickly to one side in order to avoid being hit by (someone or something)	**Dodge**
✠ Moving to a new place	**Relocate**
✠ Movement to get away from a place or situation especially because it is dangerous, unpleasant, etc ; place that is quiet and private	**Retreat**
✠ Movie about crime that uses dark shadows and lighting to show the complicated moral nature of the subject	**Noir**
✠ Mutual trust and friendship among people who spend a lot of time together	**Camaraderie**
✠ Mystery that can only be resolved by assembling various pieces of information	**Jigsaw**

- ✠ Name that is wrong or not proper or appropriate **Misnomer**
- ✠ Name that someone (such as a writer) uses instead of his or her real name **Pseudonym**
- ✠ Narrow passageway between or behind buildings **Alley**
- ✠ Natural liking for and understanding of someone or something **Affinity**
- ✠ New activity, project, business, etc, that typically involves risk **Venture**
- ✠ New and experimental ideas and methods in art, music, or literature **Avant-garde**
- ✠ Newspaper with small pages (usually half the size of those in larger papers) **Tabloid**
- ✠ Newspaper that prints a lot of shocking stories about people's private lives rather than serious news **Gutter press**
- ✠ No longer active or effective : close to failure **Moribund**
- ✠ No longer existing or being used **Defunct**
- ✠ No longer used because something newer exists **Obsolete**
- ✠ Noisy and overexcited reactions or responses to something **Brouhaha**
- ✠ Noisy argument or disagreement, especially in public **Altercation**
- ✠ Noisy arguments or fights **Fracas**
- ✠ Not able or willing to believe something **Incredulous**
- ✠ Not able to be corrected or changed **Incorrigible**
- ✠ Not able to be stopped or changed **Inexorable**
- ✠ Not able to communicate with other people **Incommunicado**

✠ Not acceptable to talk about or do	**Taboo**
✠ Not active, not now developing or causing symptoms	**Quiescent**
✠ Not as important as something else	**Subsidiary**
✠ Not capable of life	**Inanimate**
✠ Not clear in meaning ; stated in a way that is general and not specific	**Vague**
✠ Not completely clear or transparent but clear enough to allow light to pass through	**Translucent**
✠ Not connected with spiritual or religious matters	**Secular**
✠ Not deserving serious attention	**Frivolous**
✠ Not doing or involving much physical activities	**Sedentary**
✠ Not easily described ; having no special or interesting qualities, parts, etc; typical and uninteresting	**Nondescript**
✠ Not easily stopped or pulled apart; very determined to do something	**Tenacious**
✠ Not giving enough thought to other people's feelings or needs	**Inconsiderate**
✠ Not having made a will	**Intestate**
✠ Not having or showing good judgment	**Indiscreet**
✠ Not having or showing good manners, good taste, or politeness	**Vulgar**
✠ Not intended or planned	**Inadvertent**
✠ Not interesting, funny, etc, because of being used too often	**Hackneyed**
✠ Not keeping anything secret or hidden ; honest and direct	**Upfront**
✠ Not lasting long, staying somewhere only for a short time	**Transient**
✠ Not letting light through, not transparent ; difficult to understand or explain	**Opaque**
✠ Not liking to work or be active	**Indolent**

✠ Not lively or interesting ; dull or boring	**Vapid**
✠ Not made of physical substances ; not able to be touched	**Intangible**
✠ Not necessary or appropriate	**Unwarranted**
✠ Not producing the desired effect	**Inefficacious**
✠ Not showing enough care and attention	**Remiss**
✠ Not strong or stable and likely to break	**Rickety**
✠ Not very developed or advanced	**Rudimentary**
✠ Not very easy to see or notice	**Inconspicuous**
✠ Not willing to tell people about things	**Reticent**
✠ Not within the range of what someone knows or understands	**Ken**
✠ Novels, movies, etc, that are very exciting ; a story full of exciting action, mystery, adventure, or suspense	**Thriller**
✠ Number of people who are killed or injured in an accident, disaster, war	**Toll**

- ✠ Object (such as a ring or stone) that is believed to have magic powers and to cause good things to happen to the person who has it — **Talisman**
- ✠ Object or picture used to suggest a thing that cannot be shown ; a person or thing that represents an idea — **Emblem**
- ✠ Object, piece of evidence or some information that helps the police solve a crime — **Clue**
- ✠ Objects, activities, or ideas that are used as symbols of something else — **Metaphor**
- ✠ Objects or materials that are collected because they are related to a particular event, person, etc ; things collected as souvenirs — **Memorabilia**
- ✠ Objects that are used to do a particular activity ; objects of a particular kind — **Paraphernalia**
- ✠ Occurring between members of the same country, group, or organisation — **Internecine**
- ✠ Of, belonging to, or seeming to come from an early time in the very ancient past — **Primitive**
- ✠ (Of a person) not identified by name; of unknown name — **Anonymous**
- ✠ Offence of marrying someone while already married to another person — **Bigamy**
- ✠ Official agreement that is made between two or more countries or groups — **Treaty**
- ✠ Official announcement about a usually very important piece of news — **Communiqué**
- ✠ Official counting or a survey, especially of a population — **Census**

✠ Official examination of business and financial records to see that they are true and correct ; official examination of the quality or standard of something	**Audit**
✠ Official order given by a person with power or by a government	**Decree**
✠ Official order to do something ; a power to act that voters give to their elected leaders	**Mandate**
✠ Official pardon for people who have been convicted of political offences	**Amnesty**
✠ Officially cancelling the power or effect of (something, such as a law, license, agreement, etc)	**Revoke**
✠ Officially choosing (someone or something) to do or be something	**Designate**
✠ Officially preventing (someone) from leaving a place	**Detain**
✠ Officially saying that someone who is guilty of a crime will be allowed to go free and will not be punished	**Pardon**
✠ Officially stating that somebody is not responsible for something that they have been blamed for	**Exonerate**
✠ Officially telling someone to use a medicine, therapy, diet, etc as a remedy or treatment	**Prescribe**
✠ Old and respected ; valued and respected because of old age, long use, etc	**Venerable**
✠ One of a series of lives that a person is believed to have had in the past in some religions	**Incarnation**
✠ One of the official beliefs and goals of an organisation	**Plank**
✠ Open area near the entrance in someone's home	**Foyer**
✠ Open opposition toward a person or group in authority	**Rebellion**

✠ Open to more than one interpretation ; not having one obvious meaning	**Ambiguous**
✠ Operation in which police or other forces surround a building and cut off supplies, with the aim of forcing an armed person to surrender	**Siege**
✠ Opinion or belief of the majority	**Vox populi**
✠ Opponent that is easy to defeat	**Pushover**
✠ Order that must be followed	**Diktat**
✠ Organised search for a person and especially for a criminal	**Manhunt**
✠ Original copy of a play, book, piece of music, etc, before it has been printed	**Manuscript**
✠ Ornament or small piece of jewellery thought to give protection against evil, danger, or disease	**Amulet**
✠ Out of control with anger or excitement; wild or frenzied	**Berserk**
✠ Outline or outer edge of something	**Contour**
✠ Outside edge of an area ; the area that surrounds a place or thing	**Periphery**

✠ Page in newspapers opposite the editorial page that contains comment on the news and articles on particular subjects	**Op-ed**
✠ Page numbers in a printed book	**Folio**
✠ Painful emotions, sensations, or feelings	**Throes**
✠ Painting, drawing, or photograph of a person	**Portrait**
✠ Part of check, ticket, etc, that can be kept as a record when it is torn off	**Counterfoil**
✠ Part of a city in which members of a particular group or race live usually in poor conditions	**Ghetto**
✠ Part of a theatre, concert hall, etc in which the audience sits	**Auditorium**
✠ Part of the Earth's surface that is directly above the place where an earthquake starts	**Epicenter**
✠ Part of your mind that tells you whether your actions are right or wrong	**Conscience**
✠ Part or element of something	**Facet**
✠ Partial or total loss of memory	**Amnesia**
✠ Partial refunds to someone who has paid too much for tax, rent, or a utility	**Rebate**
✠ Particular subject or issue that is discussed often or repeatedly	**Theme**
✠ Particular type or category of literature or art	**Genre**
✠ Particular way of thinking ; a person's attitude or set of opinions about something	**Mindset**
✠ Particular way of walking	**Gait**
✠ Passage between rows of seats in a building such as a church or theatre, an aircraft, or train	**Aisle**

- ✠ Paying money to get a publication or service regularly **Subscribe**
- ✠ People in the future **Posterity**
- ✠ People of high social status **Gentry**
- ✠ Person who is extremely poor **Destitute**
- ✠ People who are famous, wealthy, and attractive **Glitterati**
- ✠ People who can vote in an election **Electorate**
- ✠ Performances of something **Rendition**
- ✠ Period immediately before an action or event **Run-up**
- ✠ Period of 1,000 years **Millennium**
- ✠ Period of temporary economic decline during which trade and industrial activities are reduced **Recession**
- ✠ Period of time during which someone does not work at his or her regular job and is able to rest, travel, do research, etc **Sabbatical**
- ✠ Period of time that is very important in history **Epoch**
- ✠ Period of time when people stay awake, especially at night, in order to watch a sick person, say prayers, protest, etc **Vigil**
- ✠ Period of time when something (activities or programs) is stopped **Hiatus**
- ✠ Period when the Sun has set and before it gets completely dark **Twilight**
- ✠ Period when many more babies are born than usual **Baby boom**
- ✠ Periods when something does not increase or advance any further **Plateau**
- ✠ Permanent administrative office or department, especially governmental one **Secretariat**
- ✠ Permission given to a prisoner to leave prison before the end of a sentence usually as a reward for behaving well **Parole**

✠ Person (especially a man) who leads an immoral life and is mainly interested in sexual pleasure	**Libertine**
✠ Person (such as a government official or an employee) who investigates complaints and tries to deal with problems fairly	**Ombudsman**
✠ Person and especially a man whose job is to serve meals and to take care of passengers on a train, airplane, or ship	**Steward**
✠ Person and especially a young person who causes trouble or do things that annoy people	**Rascal**
✠ Person employed in taking a census of the population	**Enumerator**
✠ Person employed to drive a private or hired car	**Chauffer**
✠ Person killed or injured in a war or accident	**Casualty**
✠ Person of roughly the same age as oneself, a contemporary	**Coeval**
✠ Person or a character in a movie, book, etc, who is very brave and has many exciting adventures	**Swashbuckler**
✠ Person or animal having a congenital absence of pigment in the skin and hair (which are white) and the eyes (which are usually pink)	**Albino**
✠ Person or animal that lives in a particular place	**Inhabitant**
✠ Person or organisation that cooperates with or helps another in a particular activity	**Ally**
✠ Person or organisation that makes sure that companies, governments, etc, are not doing anything illegal or wrong	**Watchdog**
✠ Person or a place maintained in a neat and clean condition ; well cared for	**Kempt**
✠ Person or thing regarded as an exact copy of another	**Clone**
✠ Person or thing that attracts a lot of attention or interest	**Cynosure**
✠ Person or thing that causes a change	**Catalyst**

✠ Person or thing that does not go or move as quickly as others	**Laggard**
✠ Person or thing that is connected with or related to another, often in a way that one would not expect	**Bedfellow**
✠ Person or thing that is extremely important or large in size	**Colossus**
✠ Person or thing that is the direct opposite of someone or something else	**Antithesis**
✠ Person or thing that is the most important part of an organisation, a plan, etc, because everything else depends on him/her or it	**Linchpin**
✠ Person or thing that one particularly dislikes	**Bête noire**
✠ Person or thing that takes the place of someone or something else	**Substitute**
✠ Person or thing that takes the place or performs the duties of someone or something else	**Surrogate**
✠ Person or thing which provides, stability or confidence in an otherwise uncertain situation	**Anchor**
✠ Person that somebody spends a lot of time with	**Crony**
✠ Person who accompanies and looks after another person or group of people	**Chaperone**
✠ Person who actively opposes or is hostile to someone or something ; an adversary	**Antagonist**
✠ Person who actively uses the Internet especially in a proper and responsible way	**Netizen**
✠ Person who annoys other people by correcting small errors and giving too much attention to minor details	**Pedant**
✠ Person who appreciates fine food and drink	**Epicure**
✠ Person who argues for or supports something	**Proponent**
✠ Person who behaves awkwardly around other people and usually has unstylish clothes, hair ; a person who is very interested in technical subjects, computers, etc	**Nerd**

- ✠ Person who behaves obsequiously to those in power — **Lickspittle**
- ✠ Person who behaves or reacts in an extremely or foolishly emotional way — **Hysteric**
- ✠ Person who believes that he/she has unlimited power or importance — **Megalomaniac**
- ✠ Person who buys tickets for an event and resells them at a much higher price — **Tout**
- ✠ Person who chooses to work a lot ; a person who is always working, thinking about work, etc. — **Workaholic**
- ✠ Person who compiles and analyses statistics and uses them to calculate insurance risks and premiums — **Actuary**
- ✠ Person who controls an organisation or activity — **Kingpin**
- ✠ Person who criticises or opposes beliefs and practices that are widely accepted — **Iconoclast**
- ✠ Person who criticises something or someone — **Detractor**
- ✠ Person who deliberately destroys or damages property ; a person who vandalises something — **Vandal**
- ✠ Person who does not behave the way most people behave ; someone who does not conform — **Nonconformist**
- ✠ Person who does not have experience in a particular activity, job, etc — **Virgin**
- ✠ Person who does not have expert knowledge of a particular subject — **Layman**
- ✠ Person who does not work hard — **Loafer**
- ✠ Person who does something in a very skilful way — **Virtuoso**
- ✠ Person who does something that is illegal or morally wrong — **Miscreant**
- ✠ Person who does the same thing as someone else ; a person who adopts the behaviour, style, etc, of someone else — **Copycat**
- ✠ Person who earns money to support his/her family, typically the sole one — **Breadwinner**

- ✠ Person who engages in a pursuit, especially a sport, on an unpaid basis **Amateur**
- ✠ Person who enjoys and cares about food very much **Foodie**
- ✠ Person who enjoys and knows a lot about good food and wine **Gourmet**
- ✠ Person who entices people to follow him/her in a particular course of action **Pied Piper**
- ✠ Person who follows strict moral rules and believes that pleasure is wrong **Puritan**
- ✠ Person who gives money to and supports an artist, organisation, etc **Patron**
- ✠ Person who has a sexual interest in children **Paedophile**
- ✠ Person who has broken the law and who is hiding or running away to avoid punishment **Outlaw**
- ✠ Person who has great wealth and power in a particular business or industry **Magnate**
- ✠ Person who has just started a job or activity and has little experience **Rookie**
- ✠ Person who has just started learning or doing something **Novice**
- ✠ Person who has negative opinions about other people and about the things people do **Cynic**
- ✠ Person who has no place to live and no job and who asks people for money **Vagrant**
- ✠ Person who has recently become rich and who likes to spend a lot of money **Nouveau riche**
- ✠ Person who has very strong feelings about something (such as religion or politics) and who wants other people to have those feelings **Zealot**
- ✠ Person who helps create or develop new ideas, methods, etc **Pioneer**
- ✠ Person who holds a particular office or position **Incumbent**

- Person who introduces the performers or contestants in a variety show — **Compere**
- Person who is between 40 and 49 years old — **Quadragenarian**
- Person who is between 80 and 89 years old — **Octogenarian**
- Person who is between 90 and 99 years old — **Nonagenarian**
- Person who is captured by someone who demands that certain things be done before the captured person is freed — **Hostage**
- Person who is enthusiastically interested in and very knowledgeable about a particular subject — **Buff**
- Person who is expected to save people from a very bad situation — **Messiah**
- Person who is expelled from his/her caste — **Outcaste**
- Person who is fond of or knowledgeable about the cinema — **Cineaste**
- Person who is given the power or authority to do something (such as to vote) for someone else — **Proxy**
- Person who takes part in a dialogue or conversation — **Interlocutor**
- Person who is hired to threaten, to beat up, or to kill someone — **Goon**
- Person who is in charge of or takes care of something — **Warden**
- Person who is kept in a prison or mental hospital — **Inmate**
- Person who is killed or who suffers greatly for a religion, cause, etc — **Martyr**
- Person who is not loyal to his or her own country, friends, etc — **Traitor**
- Person who is not welcome or wanted in a place — **Intruder**
- Person who is running away to avoid being captured — **Fugitive**
- Person who is sent by one government to represent it in dealing with another government — **Envoy**

✠ Person who is skilled in magic or who has magical powers ; a sorcerer or a magician, a person who is very good at something	**Wizard**
✠ Person who is unfairly blamed for something that others have done	**Scapegoat**
✠ Person who is very enthusiastic about something	**Fiend**
✠ Person who is walking in a city, along a road, etc	**Pedestrian**
✠ Person who knows a lot about something (such as art, wine, food, etc) ; an expert in a particular subject	**Connoisseur**
✠ Person who lacks experience and knowledge	**Greenhorn**
✠ Person who leaves one political, religious, etc group to join another that has very different views ; someone or something that causes trouble and cannot be controlled	**Renegade**
✠ Person who likes or admires women	**Philogynist**
✠ Person who likes seeing and talking or writing about something that is considered to be private	**Voyeur**
✠ Person who lives alone and avoids other people	**Recluse**
✠ Person who lives in a foreign country	**Expatriate**
✠ Person who lives in a simple way apart from others especially for religious reasons	**Hermit**
✠ Person who loves to eat and drink	**Gourmand**
✠ Person who makes speeches and are very good at making them	**Orator**
✠ Person who makes, does, or discovers something new and makes it acceptable or popular	**Trailblazer**
✠ Person who observes self-discipline and abstains from all forms of indulgence, typically for religious reasons	**Ascetic**
✠ Person who owns a business or property	**Proprietor**
✠ Person who owns or controls a large part of a particular industry	**Baron**
✠ Person who practises sorcery ; a wizard or warlock	**Sorcerer**

- ✠ Person who questions or doubts something (such as a claim or statement) **Sceptic**
- ✠ Person who refuses to submit to an authority or to comply with a regulation **Recusant**
- ✠ Person who sells things especially on the street **Vendor**
- ✠ Person who serves in a coffee bar **Barista**
- ✠ Person who settles a dispute or has ultimate authority in a matter **Arbiter**
- ✠ Person who shoots with a bow and arrows, especially at a target as a sport **Archer**
- ✠ Person who spends his/her time indulging in pleasure and luxury rather than dealing with practical concerns **Lotus-eater**
- ✠ Person who spoils other people's fun or enjoyment **Killjoy**
- ✠ Person who starts a business and is willing to risk loss in order to make money **Entrepreneur**
- ✠ Person who travels from place to place and does not have a home or much money **Vagabond**
- ✠ Person who wants a war or tries to make other people want to start or fight a war **Warmonger**
- ✠ Person who was born into a rich, famous, or important family **Scion**
- ✠ Person who watches an event, show, game, activity, etc, often as part of an audience **Spectator**
- ✠ Person who worships many gods or goddesses or the Earth or nature **Pagan**
- ✠ Person who writes the words of a song **Lyricist**
- ✠ Person whose job involves doing many different types of work **Factotum**
- ✠ Person whose job is to provide emergency medical care to sick or injured people who are being taken to a hospital **Paramedic**

- ✠ Person whose job is to sell eyeglasses and contact lenses, to make sure that they fit correctly, and sometimes to make eyeglasses — **Optician**
- ✠ Person whose job is to look after someone or something — **Minder**
- ✠ Person whose job is to write material for someone else who is the named author — **Ghostwriter**
- ✠ Person with whom someone is having a romantic or sexual relationship and especially a secret or improper relationship — **Paramour**
- ✠ Person, animal or plant that lives, grows or is often found in a particular place — **Denizen**
- ✠ Person, animal, or object used as a symbol to represent a group (such as a sports team) and to bring good luck — **Mascot**
- ✠ Person, business, group, etc, that pays to use another person's property — **Tenant**
- ✠ Person, company, etc, that is weak or unsuccessful and needs help — **Lame duck**
- ✠ Person, especially a lawyer, with official authority to be a witness when somebody signs a document and to make this document valid in law — **Notary**
- ✠ Person's appearance and behaviour ; the way someone seems to be to other people — **Demeanour**
- ✠ Person's secondary or alternative personality — **Alter ego**
- ✠ Person's social environment — **Milieu**
- ✠ Persuading an unwilling person to do something by using force or threats — **Coerce**
- ✠ Persuading someone gradually or gently to do something — **Coax**
- ✠ Photograph of an attractive person (such as an actress or model) that is hung or pinned on a wall — **Pin-up**
- ✠ Phrase or idea that has been used so often that it no longer has much meaning and is not interesting — **Cliché**

✠ Physical condition in which one's heart beats very quickly and in an irregular way	**Palpitation**
✠ Physical exercise in which muscles are made to work without the whole body moving	**Isometric**
✠ Picture, description or imitation of persons in which certain striking characteristics are exaggerated in order to create a comic or grotesque effect	**Caricature**
✠ Picture or word painted or drawn on a wall, building	**Graffiti**
✠ Piece of writings, music, etc, that imitates the style of someone or something else in an amusing way	**Parody**
✠ Pieces that are left after something has been destroyed	**Debris**
✠ Pithy observations which contain a general truth	**Aphorism**
✠ Placing (something) in a particular position or direction	**Orient**
✠ Place for the care and treatment of people who are recovering from illness or who have a disease that will last a long time	**Sanatorium**
✠ Place of safety and comfort	**Harbour**
✠ Place or area at which different things meet and communicate with or affect each other	**Interface**
✠ Place where a large amount of something is stored	**Repository**
✠ Place where arms are kept	**Armoury**
✠ Place where children whose parents have died can live and be cared for	**Orphanage**
✠ Place where people are buried	**Graveyard**
✠ Place where people go to improve their health and appearance by exercising, relaxing, etc	**Spa**
✠ Place where people grow fruit trees	**Orchard**

✠ Place where sick people stay and are cared for in a school, prison, summer camp	**Infirmary**
✠ Place where someone or something is protected or given shelter	**Sanctuary**
✠ Place where two rivers or streams join to become one ; situation in which two things come together or happen at the same	**Confluence**
✠ Place where two sloping surfaces meet	**Ridge**
✠ Place where you are protected from danger, trouble	**Haven**
✠ Place where you live	**Domicile**
✠ Place where young children are cared for during the day while their parents are working	**Daycare center**
✠ Plan of a journey, including the route and the places that you visit	**Itinerary**
✠ Plans or set of rules about food, exercise, etc, to make someone become or stay healthy	**Regimen**
✠ Plan which show what can be achieved and how it can be achieved	**Blueprint**
✠ Plant or animal growing or living in or near water	**Aquatic**
✠ Platform extending into an auditorium, along which models walk to display clothes in fashion shows	**Catwalk**
✠ Playing and moving about happily	**Frolic**
✠ Pleasing series of musical notes that form the main part of a song or piece of music	**Melody**
✠ Poem or song that expresses sorrow for someone who is dead	**Elegy**
✠ Poem, word puzzle, or other composition in which certain letters in each line form a word or words	**Acrostic**
✠ Point or level at which something begin or changes	**Threshold**

- ✠ Policies or practices of more open consultative government and wider dissemination of information, initiated by Russian leader Mikhail Gorbachev **Glasnost**
- ✠ Policy or system of segregation or discrimination on grounds of race **Apartheid**
- ✠ Policy that allows businesses to operate with very little interference from the government **Laissez-faire**
- ✠ Political leaders who try to get support by making false claims and promises and using arguments based on emotion rather than reason **Demagogue**
- ✠ Poor and dirty child who annoys people or causes minor trouble **Urchin**
- ✠ Popular word or phrase encapsulating a particular concept **Catchword**
- ✠ Position from which something is viewed or considered **Vantage**
- ✠ Power or right to make judgments about the law, to arrest and punish criminals **Jurisdiction**
- ✠ Power that some people are believed to have to be able to see future events **Clairvoyance**
- ✠ Practice of continuously improving the way in which a company operates **Kaizen**
- ✠ Practice or a policy of keeping people of different races, religions, etc, separate from each other **Segregation**
- ✠ Present in all places at all times **Omnipresent**
- ✠ Pressing together the parts and especially the opposite sides of something **Squeeze**
- ✠ Pressurising someone into adopting radically different beliefs by using systematic and often forcible means **Brainwash**
- ✠ Pretending to be another person **Impersonate**
- ✠ Pretending to be someone else, especially for fraudulent purposes **Personate**

- ✠ Pretending to be sick or injured in order to avoid doing work **Malinger**
- ✠ Prevailing fashion or style at a particular time **Vogue**
- ✠ Priest or minister of a religion **Clergy**
- ✠ Principles or set of principles laid down by an authority as incontrovertibly true **Dogma**
- ✠ Private conversation between two people **Tete-a-tete**
- ✠ Private or secret meetings, especially one that has special authority **Conclave**
- ✠ Problem or condition that harms or weakens a group, society **Malaise**
- ✠ Procedure carried out to improve the appearance of something **Facelift**
- ✠ Process of learning something by repeating it many times without thinking about it or fully understanding it **Rote**
- ✠ Process of making or defending a claim in court **Litigation**
- ✠ Process of reducing something's strength or effectiveness through sustained attack or pressure **Attrition**
- ✠ Process of testing or observing the character or abilities of a person who is new to a role or job **Probation**
- ✠ Producing something from available parts or elements **Cobble**
- ✠ Producing a fire ; causing anger **Incendiary**
- ✠ Promising to pay for the cost of possible damage, loss, or injury **Indemnity**
- ✠ Proof or evidence that something exists or is true **Testament**
- ✠ Property that you receive from your father when he dies **Patrimony**
- ✠ Protection granted by a state to someone who has left their native country as a political refugee **Asylum**
- ✠ Protesting or complaining about something or someone very strongly **Inveigh**

✠ Proving (something) is false by using arguments or evidence	**Rebuttal**
✠ Proverb or short statement expressing a general truth	**Adage**
✠ Providing necessary support to the primary activities or operation of an organisation, system, etc	**Ancillary**
✠ Public festival, usually one that happens at a regular time each year, that involves music and dancing in the streets, for which people wear brightly coloured clothes	**Carnival**
✠ Public performance of music	**Concert**
✠ Public sale in which goods or property are sold to the highest bidder	**Auction**
✠ Public votes on a particular issue	**Referendum**
✠ Publicly disagreeing with an official opinion, decision, or set of beliefs	**Dissent**
✠ Publicly says that you no longer have an opinion or belief that you once had	**Recant**
✠ Published collection of poems or other pieces of writing	**Anthology**
✠ Pulling something away from someone by using violent twisting movements	**Wrest**
✠ Punishment or defeat that is deserved and cannot be avoided	**Nemesis**
✠ Putting something in a secret or hidden place	**Stash**
✠ Putting people or things together, especially in order to show a contrast or a new relationship between them	**Juxtapose**

- ✠ Quality of always behaving in the same way or of having the same opinions, standard, etc — **Constituency**
- ✠ Quality of being faithful to one's husband, wife, or sexual partner — **Fidelity**
- ✠ Quality of being honest and fair — **Integrity**
- ✠ Quality of being very similar or equal — **Symmetry**
- ✠ Quality of being very unwilling to spend money — **Parsimony**
- ✠ Quality that causes people to feel sympathy and sadness — **Pathos**
- ✠ Quality that makes one person or thing different from another — **Trait**
- ✠ Quantity of work that should have been done already, but has not yet been done — **Backlog**
- ✠ Quick look or glance — **Dekko**
- ✠ Quick series of soft, light sounds caused when things (such as leaves or pieces of paper) rub against each other — **Rustle**
- ✠ Quiet and peaceful — **Tranquil**
- ✠ Quiet and polite, not showy or flashy — **Demure**
- ✠ Quotations from or references to a book, paper, or author, especially in a scholarly work — **Citation**

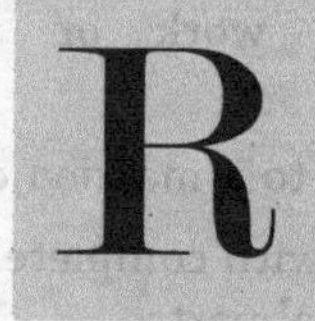

- ✠ Route or journey longer than the most direct way **Circuitous**
- ✠ Raised platform for a speaker, performer, or the leader of an orchestra **Podium**
- ✠ Raised platform in a large room or hall that people stand on when performing or speaking to an audience **Dais**
- ✠ Range or series of related things **Gamut**
- ✠ Ready and excited to start to do something **Raring**
- ✠ Reasons or explanations for something **Rationale**
- ✠ Reasons that you give to hide your real reason for doing something **Pretext**
- ✠ Records of events year by year **Annals**
- ✠ Refers to the fact that something has been done or repeated so often that it has become annoying or tiresome **Ad nauseam**
- ✠ Referring to sex in a rude but humorous way **Ribald**
- ✠ Refusing (something, such as an offer or suggestion) in a rude way **Rebuff**
- ✠ Refusing to be persuaded or to change one's mind **Adamant**
- ✠ Regular period of sleep or rest in the afternoon in some hot countries **Siesta**
- ✠ Regular, repeated patterns of sounds or movements **Rhythm**
- ✠ Reinforced underground shelters, typically for use in wartime **Bunker**
- ✠ Rejecting or refusing somebody/something, especially in a proud way **Spurn**

- ✠ Relating to a manual work or workers, particularly in industry **Blue-collar**
- ✠ Relating to a marriage or to a married couple **Conjugal**
- ✠ Relating to or concerned with complete systems rather than with individual parts **Holistic**
- ✠ Relating to or denoting exercise taken to improve the efficiency of the body's cardiovascular system in absorbing and transporting oxygen **Aerobic**
- ✠ Relating to or in the form of money **Pecuniary**
- ✠ Relating to unpleasant subjects **Morbid**
- ✠ Relationship between two different kinds of living things that live together and depend on each other **Symbiosis**
- ✠ Religious group that are a smaller part of a larger group and whose members all share similar beliefs **Sect**
- ✠ Religious leader in any religion **Cleric**
- ✠ Removing something from a place so that it will not be damaged, destroyed, or lost **Salvage**
- ✠ Repairing and make improvements to something, such as a building **Refurbish**
- ✠ Repeating something else and therefore unnecessary **Redundant**
- ✠ Replying to something in a quick and often angry way **Retort**
- ✠ Results obtained by dividing one quantity by another **Quotient**
- ✠ Returning of an illness after a period of improvement **Relapse**
- ✠ Returning to normal health or strength after being sick, injured **Recuperate**
- ✠ Returning to an earlier and usually worse state or condition **Retrograde**

- ✠ Rich person who has at least a million dollars, pounds — **Millionaire**
- ✠ Right or benefit that is given to some people and not to others — **Privilege**
- ✠ Right or the capacity to bring an action or to appear in a court — **Locus standi**
- ✠ Right or privilege — **Prerogative**
- ✠ Right to choose what should be done in a particular situation — **Discretion**
- ✠ Right to vote in an election — **Suffrage**
- ✠ Ritual suicide by cutting open one's stomach with a sword — **Hara-kiri**
- ✠ Robot with a human appearance — **Android**
- ✠ Room in a public building where outdoor clothes or luggage may be left — **Cloakroom**
- ✠ Rough or noisy — **Rowdy**
- ✠ Roughly made model of a person that is made in order to be damaged or destroyed as a protest — **Effigy**
- ✠ Roughly or quickly thrust (a sharp or pointed object) someone or something — **Jab**
- ✠ Routine tasks, especially a household one — **Chores**
- ✠ Rule or principle that most people believe to be true — **Axiom**
- ✠ Rule that says how people should behave — **Precept**
- ✠ Rule about the proper and polite way to communicate with other people when one is using the Internet — **Netiquette**

✠ Sad moods or feelings	**Melancholy**
✠ Said to somebody who is leaving on a journey, to wish them a good journey	**Bon voyage**
✠ Sailor who attacked ships at sea and stole from them ; the person who acts in a recklessly adventurous and often unscrupulous way, especially in business	**Buccaneer**
✠ Saying or writing very harsh and critical things about someone or something	**Vilify**
✠ Saying that something is smaller, less important, etc, than it really is	**Understate**
✠ Saying that something you said or wrote is not true or correct	**Retract**
✠ Saying that you are not responsible for something ; to deny that you know about or are involved in something	**Disavow**
✠ Scene full of noise and confusion	**Bedlam**
✠ Searching for something especially by moving and looking through the contents of a place	**Rummage**
✠ Searching through waste, junk, etc, for something that can be saved, used or eaten	**Scavenge**
✠ Seat for passengers on a motorcycle	**Pillion**
✠ Secret agreement especially in order to do something dishonest or to trick people	**Collusion**
✠ Secret or disguised way of writing ; a code	**Cipher**
✠ Secretly try to ruin or destroy a government, political system, etc	**Subvert**
✠ Section or table of subsidiary matter at the end of a book or document	**Appendix**

- ✠ Seeming like real life because it is very clear, bright, or detailed, very bright in colour — **Vivid**
- ✠ Seeming to be seen everywhere — **Ubiquitous**
- ✠ Selling (a business, property, etc) especially to pay off debt — **Liquidate**
- ✠ Sending a person who has been accused of a crime to another state or country for trial — **Extradite**
- ✠ Sending away some of a company's work to be done by people outside the company — **Outsource**
- ✠ Series of changes — **Flux**
- ✠ Series of three novels, movies, etc, that are closely related and involve the same characters or themes — **Trilogy**
- ✠ Set of clothes that are worn together ; group of people working together in the same activity — **Outfit**
- ✠ Set of ideas that somebody believes in and tries to persuade others to accept — **Gospel**
- ✠ Set of principles concerned with the nature and appreciation of beauty — **Aesthetics**
- ✠ Set of tools or supplies that a person uses for a particular purpose or activity — **Kit**
- ✠ Severe mental or physical pain or suffering — **Anguish**
- ✠ Severe snowstorm with high winds ; large quantity of things that may seem to be attacking you — **Blizzard**
- ✠ Sexually attracted to people of the same sex — **Homosexual**
- ✠ Shared by, including or typical of a whole group of things ; not specific — **Generic**
- ✠ Shiny quality of a surface that reflects light — **Luster**
- ✠ Short amusing or interesting story about a real incident or person — **Anecdote**
- ✠ Short and clever poem or saying — **Epigram**
- ✠ Short argument about something that is not important — **Spat**

✠ Short break or escape from something difficult or unpleasant	**Respite**
✠ Short description of a book, film, or other product written for promotional purpose	**Blurb**
✠ Short description of the most important information about something	**Synopsis**
✠ Short journeys that you take to do or get something	**Errand**
✠ Short period of greatly increased efforts, activities, or developments	**Spurt**
✠ Short period of time during which something lasts ; the quality that a person or thing has that makes him/her so attractive or interesting that he/she has a strong influence on you	**Spell**
✠ Short period of time when you do a lot of something	**Spree**
✠ Short sleep during the day	**Catnap**
✠ Short story that teaches a moral or a spiritual lesson	**Parable**
✠ Short story that usually is about animals and that is intended to teach a lesson	**Fable**
✠ Short trip especially for pleasure	**Excursion**
✠ Short written description	**Vignette**
✠ Short, funny stories or performances	**Skit**
✠ Short, well-known pithy sayings, stating a general truth or piece of advice	**Proverb**
✠ Shot that comes from two or more places so that the bullets cross through the same area	**Crossfire**
✠ Showing somebody in authority too much respect and be too willing to obey them	**Kowtow**
✠ Showing that someone or something that has been criticised or doubted is correct, true, or reasonable	**Vindicate**

- ✠ Showing a loss of mental ability (such as memory) in old age — **Senile**
- ✠ Showing no emotion especially when something bad is happening — **Stoical**
- ✠ Showing no feeling or emotion ; humour that is done or said in a serious way — **Deadpan**
- ✠ Showing or having very little strength, energy, or activity — **Languid**
- ✠ Showing strong and often angry feelings — **Vehement**
- ✠ Silly or childish, especially in a way that shows a lack of seriousness or good judgment — **Puerile**
- ✠ Sitting on heels with one's knees bent up close to the body ; live in a building or on land which is not yours ; without the owner's permission — **Squat**
- ✠ Situation characterised by instability and strong emotions — **Cauldron**
- ✠ Situation in which a relationship becomes more friendly and less angry — **Thaw**
- ✠ Situation in which everyone is treated equally ; shares in a company which do not pay a fixed amount of interest — **Equity**
- ✠ Situation in which many people are upset, angry, or disturbed by something — **Uproar**
- ✠ Situation in which many people leave a place at the same time — **Exodus**
- ✠ Situation in which no progress can be made — **Gridlock**
- ✠ Situation in which there is much noise, confusion, excitement, and activity — **Hubbub**
- ✠ Situation in which two people or groups argue or compete with each other — **Duel**
- ✠ Situation in which you are confused about what to do — **Quandary**

- ✠ Situation in which one is forced to leave one's country or home and go to live in a foreign country **Exile**
- ✠ Situation in which one has to make a difficult choice **Dilemma**
- ✠ Situations or events which are much less impressive than expected **Damp squib**
- ✠ Situation or series of events in which people have very strong or exaggerated emotions **Melodrama**
- ✠ Situation or way of behaving that does not change **Rut**
- ✠ Situation when both players have 40 as a score **Deuce**
- ✠ Situation which creates a sudden increase in wealth, good fortune, or profits **Bonanza**
- ✠ Skill and cleverness that is shown in the way someone deals with a situation, problem, etc **Finesse**
- ✠ Slowing down the development or progress of something **Retard**
- ✠ Slow in moving, acting, or happening **Tardy**
- ✠ Slowly decay or cause (something) to decay **Rot**
- ✠ Small book or magazine containing pictures and information about a product or service **Brochure**
- ✠ Small but noticeable part in a play or film, played by a distinguished actor **Cameo**
- ✠ Small close-knit group of people who do not readily allow others to join them **Clique**
- ✠ Small dish of food or a drink taken before a meal or the main course of a meal to stimulate one's appetite **Appetizer**
- ✠ Small group of people who are interested in the same thing and who usually do not allow other people to join the group **Coterie**
- ✠ Small part of a longer written work **Excerpt**
- ✠ Small piece of news or interesting information ; small piece of food **Titbit**

✠ Small pointed objects, sometimes with feathers to help it fly, that is shot as a weapon	**Dart**
✠ Small raised platform on a stage	**Rostrum**
✠ Small room, especially one used for storing things or for private study	**Closet**
✠ Small shop selling fashionable clothes or accessories	**Boutique**
✠ Small store in a building or on the street where things (such as newspapers or candy) are sold	**Kiosk**
✠ Small stream	**Brook**
✠ Small waterfall, typically one of several that fall in stages down a steep rocky slope	**Cascade**
✠ Small, somewhat soft part inside a seed or nut ; very small amount of something	**Kernel**
✠ Small, usually round pieces of food	**Nugget**
✠ Smaller earthquake following the main shock of a large earthquake	**Aftershock**
✠ Soldiers who are paid by a foreign country to fight in its army	**Mercenary**
✠ Solemn patriotic song officially adopted by a country as an expression of national identity	**Anthem**
✠ Someone (such as a member of a religious group) who lives by asking people for money or food	**Mendicant**
✠ Someone or something that causes a great amount of trouble or suffering	**Scourge**
✠ Someone or something that causes bad luck	**Jinx**
✠ Someone or something that gives a feeling of comfort to a person who is sad, depressed, etc ; a source of comfort	**Solace**
✠ Someone or something that has the same name as another person or thing	**Namesake**
✠ Someone or something that has the typical qualities of a particular group, kind, etc	**Prototype**

- ✠ Someone or something that is difficult to understand or explain **Enigma**
- ✠ Someone or something that is getting started in a new activity **Fledgling**
- ✠ Someone or something that will not be effective or successful **Non-starter**
- ✠ Someone who achieves success or shows great talent at a young age - usually singular **Wunderkind**
- ✠ Someone who has been forced to leave a country because of war or for religious or political reasons **Refugee**
- ✠ Someone who has won an important prize or honour for achievement in a subject of study **Laureate**
- ✠ Someone who is guilty of a crime or offence ; a person whose behaviour is wrong or evil **Malefactor**
- ✠ Someone who is not accepted by other people **Outcast**
- ✠ Someone who is not accepted or welcome by other people **Persona nongrata**
- ✠ Someone who is not powerful or important and who obeys the orders of a powerful leader or boss **Minion**
- ✠ Someone who makes a bet **Punter**
- ✠ Someone who makes predictions about what is going to happen in the future **Soothsayer**
- ✠ Someone who predicts things that will happen in the future **Seer**
- ✠ Someone who saves something or someone from danger, harm, failure, etc **Saviour**
- ✠ Someone who supports a particular cause, belief, etc **Exponent**
- ✠ Someone who talks about something with great enthusiasm **Evangelist**
- ✠ Someone who teaches or gives help and advice to a less experienced and often younger person **Mentor**

✠ Someone who tends to criticise, reject, or ignore people who come from a lower social class and have less education, etc	**Snob**
✠ Someone who travels to a holy place	**Pilgrim**
✠ Someone who tries to get an advantage or something valuable from a situation without thinking about what is fair or right	**Opportunist**
✠ (Something unwelcome) flourishing or spreading unchecked, unrestrained in action or performance	**Rampant**
✠ Something (such as a business) that develops from something larger	**Offshoot**
✠ Something (such as a force, campaign, or movement) that is extremely large and powerful and cannot be stopped	**Juggernaut**
✠ Something (such as a greeting) that people say in order to be polite	**Pleasantry**
✠ Something (such as a situation) that is made up of two opposite things and that seems impossible but is actually true or possible	**Paradox**
✠ Something (such as a special ceremony) that is intended to honour an important event or person from the past	**Commemoration**
✠ Something (such as a speech or a piece of writing) that praises someone or something	**Panegyric**
✠ Something (such as an interest or fashion) that is very popular for a short time	**Fad**
✠ Something (such as salt, mustard, or ketchup) that is added to food to give it more flavour	**Condiment**
✠ Something bad that might happen in the future	**Spectre**
✠ Something extra that someone receives in addition to regular pay for doing a job	**Perk**
✠ Something heard from another person	**Hearsay**
✠ Something or someone that one vehemently dislikes	**Anathema**

- ✠ Something said or done to cause laughter **Jest**
- ✠ Something that comes before and leads to something else **Prelude**
- ✠ Something that comes before something else and that often leads to or influences its development **Precursor**
- ✠ Something that deviates from what is standard, normal, or expected **Anomaly**
- ✠ Something that does not have much value or importance **Trifle**
- ✠ Something that does not really exist **Figment**
- ✠ Something that has been done and cannot be changed **Fait accompli**
- ✠ Something that involves many quickly changing events, feelings, etc **Whirlwind**
- ✠ Something that is absolutely needed **Sine qua non**
- ✠ Something that is believed to be a sign or warning of something that will happen in the future **Omen**
- ✠ Something that is boring because it is always the same **Monotonous**
- ✠ Something that is done or given to someone in order to prevent trouble, gain support, etc **Sop**
- ✠ Something that is done to honour someone or something **Homage**
- ✠ Something that is done too much and in a wild way **Orgy**
- ✠ Something that is done without energy or enthusiasm because of habit or because it is expected **Perfunctory**
- ✠ Something that is from a past time, place, culture, etc **Relic**
- ✠ Something that is given for free **Freebie**
- ✠ Something that is given to you or done for you in return for something you have given to or done for someone else **Quid pro quo**

✠ Something that is intended to make a bad situation seem better but that does not really improve the situation	**Palliative**
✠ Something that is kept as a reminder of a person, place, or thing	**Memento**
✠ Something that is known or understood without proof or evidence	**Intuition**
✠ Something that is made by combining different things (such as ideas, styles, etc)	**Synthesis**
✠ Something that is necessary in a particular situation	**Exigency**
✠ Something that is pleasing and well chosen	**Felicity**
✠ Something that is regarded as true	**Verity**
✠ Something that is shocking, upsetting, or ridiculous because it is not what it is supposed to be	**Travesty**
✠ Something that is sure to happen	**Inevitable**
✠ Something that is too expensive	**Rip-off**
✠ Something that naturally follows or results from another thing	**Corollary**
✠ Something that people are not supposed to do because it is not proper, safe, fashionable, etc	**No-no**
✠ Something that people use to express their emotions or talents	**Outlet**
✠ Something that seems real but does not really exist	**Hallucination**
✠ Something that shows what is coming	**Harbinger**
✠ Something that someone says especially in a court of law while formally promising to tell the truth	**Testimony**
✠ Something that will solve all problems	**Panacea**
✠ Something that you do or are given to do in order to show that you are sad or sorry about doing something wrong	**Penance**

✠ Something that you do or give to help someone who is suffering or in a difficult situation	**Succor**
✠ Something that you hope for or want but that is not possible or real	**Mirage**
✠ Something that you officially must have or do before you can have or do something else	**Prerequisite**
✠ Something that you say, give, or do to show respect or affection for someone	**Tribute**
✠ Something very pleasing to taste or smell	**Ambrosia**
✠ Something very successful, especially a very successful book or film/movie	**Blockbuster**
✠ Something written or said in memory of a dead person ; especially words written on a gravestone	**Epitaph**
✠ Something, typically money, awarded to someone in recognition of loss, suffering, or injury	**Compensation**
✠ Song of joy, praise, or victory	**Paean**
✠ Song or poem that tells a story	**Ballad**
✠ Song that praises God	**Hymn**
✠ Song used to help a child fall asleep	**Lullaby**
✠ Source of many troubles ; something that will lead to many problems	**Pandora's box**
✠ Space or room inside or partly inside the roof of a building	**Attic**
✠ Speaking in a very high voice, especially when one is excited or nervous	**Squeal**
✠ Speaking in an angry and critical way to (someone who has done something wrong, disobeyed an order, etc)	**Reprimand**
✠ Speaking or performing without previously preparing one's words	**Ad lib**
✠ Speaking or writing about something in a way that includes a lot of details or uses many words	**Expatiate**
✠ Speaking quickly or in a confused way because one is upset, surprised, etc	**Sputter**

- ✠ Speaking very softly or quietly **Whisper**
- ✠ Speaking with many pauses and repetitions because one has a speech problem or because one is very nervous, frightened, etc **Stammer**
- ✠ Special anniversary ; also a celebration at the time of such an anniversary **Jubilee**
- ✠ Special buildings made to hold the dead body of an important person or the dead bodies of a family **Mausoleum**
- ✠ Special clothes and decorations (such as a crown or scepter) for official ceremonies **Regalia**
- ✠ Special protection from what is required for most people by law **Immunity**
- ✠ Special show or performance that allows some people to see a movie, play, etc **Preview**
- ✠ Species of human beings that exists today ***Homo sapiens***
- ✠ Spectacular gymnastic feats **Acrobatics**
- ✠ Speech about a moral or religious subject that is usually given by a religious leader **Sermon**
- ✠ Speech that praises someone who has died **Eulogy**
- ✠ Speech, etc at the end of a play, book, or film/movie that comments on or acts as a conclusion to what has happened **Epilogue**
- ✠ Spending time with someone (such as a famous or wealthy person) in a friendly way **Hobnob**
- ✠ Spoken or done without preparation **Extempore**
- ✠ Standards or points of reference against which things may be compared **Benchmark**
- ✠ Standards of proper or acceptable behaviour **Norm**
- ✠ Starting a motorcycle by pushing down on a lever with one's foot **Kick-start**
- ✠ Starting, stopping, and starting again **Intermittent**

- ✠ State in which someone (such as a person who has been surprised or injured) is not able to think or act normally — **Daze**
- ✠ State in which one is not aware of what is happening around because he or she is thinking of something else — **Trance**
- ✠ State of abstaining from marriage and sexual relations — **Celibacy**
- ✠ State of balance, especially between opposing forces or influences ; calm state of mind and a balance of emotions — **Equilibrium**
- ✠ State of being full of life or vigour ; liveliness — **Animation**
- ✠ State of being in someone's power, or of having great power over someone — **Thrall**
- ✠ State of being married ; marriage — **Matrimony**
- ✠ State of being very tired — **Fatigue**
- ✠ State of confusion or disorder — **Turmoil**
- ✠ State of continuing forever or for a very long time — **Perpetuity**
- ✠ State of disorder due to absence or non-recognition of authority or other controlling systems — **Anarchy**
- ✠ State of limited competition, in which a market is shared by a small number of producers or sellers — **Oligopoly**
- ✠ State or feeling of great happiness, pleasure, or love — **Rapture**
- ✠ State or period of sadness or depression — **Doldrums**
- ✠ State or practice of being married to more than one person at the same time — **Polygamy**
- ✠ Statement or address made at or as a farewell — **Valediction**
- ✠ Statement that is accepted as being true and that is used as the basis of a theory, argument, etc — **Postulate**
- ✠ Statement that is made at the beginning of something (such as a legal document) and usually gives the reasons for the parts that follow — **Preamble**

- ✠ Statement that is not connected in a logical or clear way to anything said before it **Non sequitur**
- ✠ Statement to be proved, explained, or discussed **Proposition**
- ✠ Statement which indirectly suggests that someone has done something immoral, improper **Innuendo**
- ✠ Statues or structures established to remind people of a person or event **Memorial**
- ✠ Stock markets in a non-English-speaking country, especially France **Bourse**
- ✠ Stopping someone from doing something or to stop something from happening **Stymie**
- ✠ Stopping in trying to resist something, die **Succumb**
- ✠ Stories from the past that are believed by many people but cannot be proved to be true ; famous or important persons who are known for doing something extremely well **Legend**
- ✠ Story or event with a strong element of suspense **Cliffhanger**
- ✠ Strange because of not agreeing with what is usual or expected **Incongruous**
- ✠ Stream that flows into a larger stream or river or into a lake **Tributary**
- ✠ Strength of spirit ; ability to continue despite difficulties **Mettle**
- ✠ Strength, energy, or determination **Vigour**
- ✠ Strong and full of energy, especially sexual energy **Virile**
- ✠ Strong and unusual needs or desires for something **Fetish**
- ✠ Strong and violent person (especially a man) who threatens and hurts other people **Ruffian**
- ✠ Strong base for something, especially the facts or the principles on which it is based **Bedrock**

- ✠ Strong belief that one's own country is best, especially when this is expressed in support of war with another country **Jingoism**
- ✠ Strong desire for money or possessions **Cupidity**
- ✠ Strong feeling of anger towards someone that lasts for a long time **Grudge**
- ✠ Strong feeling of interest and enthusiasm that makes someone very eager or determined to do something **Zeal**
- ✠ Strong feeling that something is about to happen, especially something unpleasant **Premonition**
- ✠ Strong negative reaction by a large number of people, for example to something that has recently changed in society **Backlash**
- ✠ Strong or violent attack **Onslaught**
- ✠ Strong sense of happiness, power, or importance **Exaltation**
- ✠ Strong written or spoken attack against someone else's opinions, beliefs, practices, etc **Polemic**
- ✠ Strongest or most successful period of time **Zenith**
- ✠ Structures on which a criminal who has been sentenced to death is killed by being hanged **Gallows**
- ✠ Struggle between two people or groups to win control or possession of something **Tug of war**
- ✠ Students in the second year of high school or college **Sophomore**
- ✠ Students or recent graduates who work for a period of time at a job in order to get experience **Intern**
- ✠ Students who miss school without permission **Truant**
- ✠ Study of how to speak clearly and in a way that is effective and socially acceptable **Elocution**
- ✠ Study or collection of postage stamps **Philately**
- ✠ Study very hard for an exam **Swot**
- ✠ Stupid person **Dimwit**

✠ Style of dancing that tells a dramatic story with music but no talking or singing	**Ballet**
✠ Subjects that are included in a course of study or taught in a school, college, etc	**Curriculum**
✠ Sudden attack in which a group of soldiers rush forward against an enemy	**Sortie**
✠ Sudden expressions of strong feeling, sudden increase in activity	**Outburst**
✠ Sudden feelings of annoyance or anger when someone has offended you	**Pique**
✠ Sudden invasion or attack, attempt to do something especially for the first time, short journey	**Foray**
✠ Sudden occurrence of applause, laughter, etc, from many people	**Salvo**
✠ Sudden rapid movements or reactions of a mass of people in response to a particular circumstance or stimulus	**Stampede**
✠ Sudden reversal of fortune or change in circumstances	**Peripeteia**
✠ Sudden sharp drop in price, value, condition, etc	**Nosedive**
✠ Sudden start or increase of fighting or disease	**Outbreak**
✠ Sudden violent political or social upheavals	**Cataclysm**
✠ Sudden violent rainstorm	**Cloudburst**
✠ Sudden, dramatic, and important discoveries or developments	**Breakthrough**
✠ Suddenly increasing to an unusually high level	**Surge**
✠ Suffer or die from lack of food ; to suffer extreme hunger	**Starve**
✠ Sum of money advanced to a person for a particular purpose	**Imprest**
✠ Surprise attack by people lying in wait in a concealed position	**Ambush**

✠ Surprising or frightening someone suddenly and usually not seriously	**Startle**
✠ Suspending a student from a university as a punishment	**Rusticate**
✠ Symbol (such as a number or letter) written above and immediately to the left or right of another character	**Superscript**
✠ Symbol, badge or sign that shows somebody's rank or that he/she is a member of a group or an organisation	**Insignia**
✠ System of marks, signs, figures, or characters that is used to represent information	**Notation**
✠ System of names for things especially in science	**Nomenclature**
✠ System of politics based on a country's situation and its needs rather than on ideas about what is morally right and wrong	**Realpolitik**
✠ System of rules that explain the correct conduct and procedures to be followed in formal situations	**Protocol**
✠ System of underground trains in a city	**Subway**
✠ System (especially in a society or an organisation) in which people are organised into different levels of importance from highest to lowest	**Hierarchy**

- ✠ Table or device designed to assist with calculation **Reckoner**
- ✠ Taking money or property from (someone) by using lies or tricks **Swindle**
- ✠ Taking or moving (someone or something) somewhere suddenly and quickly **Whisk**
- ✠ Taking the place of someone or something that is old, no longer useful, etc ; to replace someone or something **Supersede**
- ✠ Taking things from a place, such as a city or town by force especially during a war, to loot or plunder a place **Pillage**
- ✠ Taking too long to do something ; go somewhere or make a decision **Dilly-dally**
- ✠ Taking place every other year **Biennial**
- ✠ Talking for very long about something that is not important or interesting **Prattle**
- ✠ Talking loudly and in a way that shows anger **Rant**
- ✠ Talking or writing about someone or something in an excited or enthusiastic way **Rave**
- ✠ Talking with an enemy or someone you disagree with especially in order to end a conflict **Parley**
- ✠ Talking in a free and honest way about one's opinions **Outspoken**
- ✠ Taxes on goods coming into or leaving a country **Tariff**
- ✠ Taxes or payments of an equal amount for each person; the system of payments of this kind **Capitation**
- ✠ Temporary suspension of fighting ; a truce **Ceasefire**
- ✠ Tending to be quiet ; not speaking frequently **Taciturn**

✠ That can be done ; that will be successful	**Viable**
✠ The last of a series	**Omega**
✠ The same book or piece of writing as the one that has just been mentioned	**Ibid**
✠ The thing added to something else as a supplementary rather than an essential part	**Adjunct**
✠ The thing or a person that has no chance of success	**Noose**
✠ The thing that existed before or logically precedes another	**Antecedent**
✠ The thing that hides or covers somebody/something	**Cloak**
✠ The thing that is added or attached to something larger or more important	**Appendage**
✠ The thing that is inappropriate, especially a remark or expression	**Infelicity**
✠ The thing that is most important to someone or something	**Raison detre**
✠ The time at which something begins	**Inception**
✠ The time that something of quality was produced	**Vintage**
✠ The traditional knowledge, beliefs, and stories that relate to a particular place, subject, or group	**Lore**
✠ The treatment to improve the appearance and health of the feet or toenails	**Pedicure**
✠ The trusted follower or supporter who performs unpleasant, wrong, or illegal tasks for a powerful person	**Henchman**
✠ The two-hundredth anniversary of a significant event	**Bicentenary**
✠ Theories or a group of ideas about how something should be done, made, or thought about	**Paradigm**
✠ Thick and deep mud	**Mire**

✠ Thick cloud of very small drops of water in the air close to the land or sea, that is very difficult to see through ; state of confusion, in which things are not clear	**Fog**
✠ Thick mass of coagulated liquid, especially blood, or of material stuck together	**Clot**
✠ Thing to be corrected, typically error in a printed book	**Corrigendum**
✠ Thing with distinct and independent existence	**Entity**
✠ Thing that is brought into or out of a country illegally	**Contraband**
✠ Thing that is done to find out secrets from enemies or competitors	**Espionage**
✠ Thinking about something and make guesses about it ; invest money in a way that could produce a large profit but that also involves a lot of risk	**Speculate**
✠ Thinking carefully and deeply about something	**Ruminate**
✠ Thinking clearly or act sensibly	**Brainstorm**
✠ Time during which something stops or slows down	**Let-up**
✠ Tired and bored, usually because one has had too much of something	**Jaded**
✠ Title for a priest or minister in the Christian church	**Reverend**
✠ Title or brief explanation accompanying an illustration, cartoon, or poster	**Caption**
✠ To kill or destroy (someone or something) by fire	**Immolation**
✠ To touch or push (someone or something) gently	**Nudge**
✠ To transmit (a programme or some information) by radio or television	**Broadcast**
✠ To travel by asking for free rides in other people's cars	**Hitchhike**

✠ To try to end a disagreement between two or more people or groups by talking to them	**Mediate**
✠ To twist from side to side with small quick movements like a worm	**Wriggle**
✠ Too confident about oneself in a way that annoys other people	**Cocky**
✠ Too eager to help or obey someone important	**Obsequious**
✠ Too emotional or dramatic	**Histrionic**
✠ Too great, powerful, beautiful, etc, to be described or expressed	**Ineffable**
✠ Too important and respected to be changed, criticised, etc	**Sacrosanct**
✠ Too much of something ; a supply of something that is much more than is needed or wanted	**Glut**
✠ Too much pride in one's own appearance, abilities or achievements	**Vanity**
✠ Transparent tanks of water in which live fish and other water creatures and plants are kept	**Aquarium**
✠ Travelling regularly to and from a place and especially between where you live and where you work	**Commute**
✠ Trick or plan for deceiving an enemy or for achieving a goal	**Stratagem**
✠ Twist and squeeze (wet cloth, hair, etc) to remove water	**Wring**
✠ Type of lively dance	**Jig**
✠ Typical example of a certain person or thing	**Archetype**

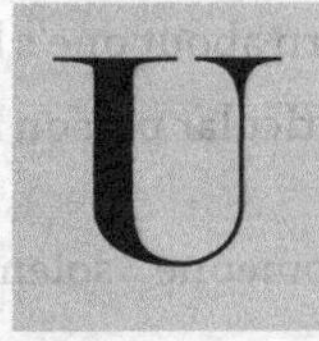

- ✠ Unable to move **Inert**
- ✠ Unambiguously explicit and direct **Categorical**
- ✠ Unattractive or unpleasant persons or things **Minger**
- ✠ Under judicial consideration and therefore prohibited from public discussion elsewhere **Subjudice**
- ✠ Undercarriage with four or six wheels pivoted beneath the end of a railway vehicle **Bogie**
- ✠ Undeveloped sites for commercial development or exploitation **Greenfield**
- ✠ Unexpected and inexplicable changes in a situation or in someone's behaviour **Vagary**
- ✠ Unexpected and usually minor problem **Glitch**
- ✠ Unexpected or unusual thing that happens by accident **Fluke**
- ✠ Unfashionable or socially inept person **Geek**
- ✠ Unfounded rumour or story **Canard**
- ✠ University, school, or college that one formerly attended **Alma mater**
- ✠ Unmarried woman who is past the usual age for marrying and is considered unlikely to marry **Spinster**
- ✠ Unpleasant and unkind talk about somebody who is not present **Backbiting**
- ✠ Unreasonable feeling that people are trying to harm you, do not like you, etc **Paranoia**
- ✠ Unskilful doctor or a person who falsely claims to have medical skills **Quack**
- ✠ Unusual habit or way of behaving, something strange that happens by chance **Quirk**

- ✠ Unusual or excessive concern about one's health **Hypochondria**
- ✠ Unusual way in which a particular person behaves or thinks **Idiosyncrasy**
- ✠ Urging or requesting someone solemnly or earnestly to do something **Adjure**
- ✠ Using something in a foolish or wasteful way **Squander**
- ✠ Use of deception or subterfuge to achieve one's purpose **Chicanery**
- ✠ Use of machines to do work that was previously done by people **Automation**
- ✠ Use of many words where fewer would do, especially in a deliberate attempt to be vague or evasive **Circumlocution**
- ✠ Use of tricks especially to hide, avoid, or get something **Subterfuge**
- ✠ Use of words that mean the opposite of what one really wants to say especially in order to insult someone, to show irritation, or to be funny **Sarcasm**
- ✠ Use of words to exchange thoughts and ideas **Discourse**
- ✠ Used in reference to luxurious accommodations **Ritz**
- ✠ Used to describe something that exists but that is not officially accepted or recognised **De facto**
- ✠ Used to express excitement or joy **Yahoo**
- ✠ Used to express excitement when a discovery has been made **Eureka**
- ✠ Used to indicate that a named person is also known or more familiar under another specified name **Alias**
- ✠ Used to refer to a process in which actors are chosen for a film/movie, etc if they have sex with the person in charge of choosing the actors **Casting couch**
- ✠ Used to say the opposite of what one has just said **Vice versa**
- ✠ Using few words in speech or writing **Laconic**

- ✠ Using forceful methods to make others do what you want them to do ; aggressive and rude — **Pushy**
- ✠ Usually artificial lake that is used to store a large supply of water for use in people's homes, in businesses, etc ; extra supply of something — **Reservoir**
- ✠ Usually large amount of money won in a game of chance — **Jackpot**
- ✠ Usually a rude or angry reply to something written or said — **Rejoinder**
- ✠ Usually small amount of money that is paid regularly to someone — **Stipend**
- ✠ Usually a violent attempt to take control of a government — **Insurgency**
- ✠ Usually a violent attempt to take control of a government — **Insurrection**
- ✠ Usually a violent effort by many people to change the government or leader of a country — **Uprising**
- ✠ Usually a young man who does noisy and violent things as part of a group or gang — **Hooligan**
- ✠ Uttered at the end of a prayer or hymn, meaning 'so be it' — **Amen**

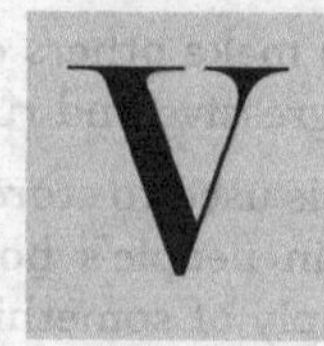

✠ Victory won at too great a cost	**Pyrrhic**
✠ Valuable stolen goods, especially those seized in war	**Booty**
✠ Various forms in which the atoms of a chemical element can occur	**Isotope**
✠ Very angry or violent disagreement between two or more people or groups	**Strife**
✠ Very bad ; causing great fear or worry	**Dire**
✠ Very bad or frightening experience or situation	**Nightmare**
✠ Very big and powerful company or organisation	**Behemoth**
✠ Very careful about behaving properly and doing things in a correct and accurate way	**Punctilious**
✠ Very careful about doing something in an extremely accurate and exact way	**Meticulous**
✠ Very close to being something without actually being it	**Virtual**
✠ Very comfortable and expensive	**Opulent**
✠ Very complicated and difficult to understand	**Turgid**
✠ Very determined or loyal	**Diehard**
✠ Very different, strange, or unusual	**Exotic**
✠ Very dirty and unpleasant, immoral or dishonest	**Squalid**
✠ Very dirty or untidy state or condition	**Mess**
✠ Very eager or curious to hear or see something	**Agog**
✠ Very excited or upset	**Overwrought**
✠ Very famous or successful person	**Luminary**
✠ Very hard to please, requiring a lot of care or attention	**Finicky**

✠ Very large and exciting shows or events	**Extravaganza**
✠ Very large and impressive ; like a palace	**Palatial**
✠ Very large building or other structure	**Monolith**
✠ Very large city, area that includes a large city or several large cities	**Megapolis**
✠ Very large or important city	**Metropolis**
✠ Very long and violent fights between two families or groups	**Vendetta**
✠ Very loud sound that comes from the sky during a storm	**Thunder**
✠ Very nervous feelings	**Jitter**
✠ Very obedient and trying too hard to please someone	**Servile**
✠ Very offensive in usually a shocking way	**Obscene**
✠ Very old or old-fashioned	**Archaic**
✠ Very silly or stupid	**Inane**
✠ Very skilful and successful effort or performance	**Tour de force**
✠ Very small amount of money	**Pittance**
✠ Very small amount	**Scrap**
✠ Very small difference in colour, tone, meaning, etc	**Nuance**
✠ Very small village	**Hamlet**
✠ Very strong, clear, and effective	**Trenchant**
✠ Very unhappy, ill, etc ; very poor in quality or ability ; very bad or unpleasant	**Wretched**
✠ Very upset ; so upset that one is not able to think clearly or behave normally	**Distraught**
✠ Very wealthy and powerful business person	**Tycoon**
✠ Very willing or too willing to obey someone else	**Subservient**
✠ Very young children	**Tot**
✠ View or sight that looks like a picture	**Tableau**

- Vigorous and pioneering advocates or supporters of a particular policy, idea, or cause **Apostle**
- Violent killing of many people **Massacre**
- Voluntarily giving of help, typically in the form of money, to those in need **Charity**
- Voluntary sexual intercourse between a married person and a person who is not his/her spouse **Adultery**
- Vote by which the people of a country or region express their opinion for or against an important proposal **Plebiscite**

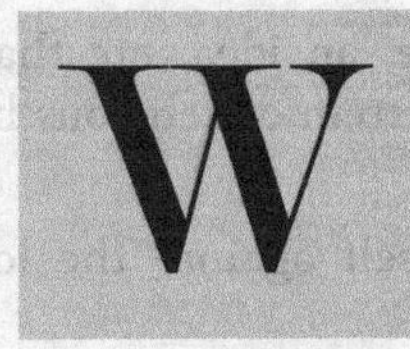

- Walking along in a slow and relaxed manner **Saunter**
- Walking along or across a street illegally or without paying attention to the traffic **Jaywalk**
- Walking for a long distance or time **Tramp**
- Walking on or along (something) **Tread**
- Walking or moving at a slow, relaxed pace **Amble**
- Walking or moving slowly as you follow behind (someone or something) **Trail**
- Walking slowly and heavily because one is tired or working very hard **Trudge**
- Walking slowly and usually heavily **Plod**
- Walking with very long steps **Stride**
- Walking with your heels raised up and only your toes touching the ground **Tiptoe**
- Warning or proviso of specific stipulations, conditions, or limitations **Caveat**
- Way in which somebody/something appears, often in a way that is different from usual or that hides the truth about he/she/it **Guise**
- Way of appearing or behaving that is not true or real **Masquerade**
- Way of behaving, proceeding, etc, that is developing and becoming more common **Tendency**
- Way of communicating thoughts directly from one person's mind to another person's mind without using words or signals **Telepathy**

✠ Way of life, an attitude, an idea, etc that has become very popular, system of religious beliefs and rituals	**Cult**
✠ Way of protecting oneself against the loss of something	**Hedge**
✠ Way that a person thinks about things	**Outlook**
✠ Way that a room or the inside of a building is decorated	**Décor**
✠ Way that prevents other people from finding out who you are	**Incognito**
✠ Wealthy person who gives money and time to help make life better for other people	**Philanthropist**
✠ Well-known phrases that express a general truth about life or a rule about behaviour	**Maxim**
✠ Wild and drunken celebration	**Bacchanal**
✠ Wild and noisy celebrations	**Revelry**
✠ Willing to do dishonest things in return for money	**Venal**
✠ Wise, skilled, and respected government leaders	**Statesman**
✠ Without a future date being arranged	**Sine die**
✠ Woman who controls a family, group, or government	**Matriarch**
✠ Woman who has control or power over others	**Mistress**
✠ Woman who is paid to care for a young child usually in the child's home	**Nanny**
✠ Woman who is thought to have magic powers	**Witch**
✠ Woman who uses her sexual charm to make men do what she wants	**Vamp**
✠ Woman who works in a bar, serving drinks	**Bartender**
✠ Woman whose job is to be in charge of children or other woman	**Matron**
✠ Woman's male lover or friend	**Beau**

✠ Woman's underwear and clothing that is worn in bed	**Lingerie**
✠ Word opposite in meaning to another	**Antonym**
✠ Word or phrase, often an item of jargon, that is fashionable at a particular time or in a particular context	**Buzzword**
✠ Word that is spelled and pronounced like another word but is different in meaning	**Homonym**
✠ Word, name, or expression used as a substitute for something else with which those are closely associated	**Metonym**
✠ Word, phrase, or name formed by rearranging the letters of another, such as *spar,* formed from *rasp*	**Anagram**
✠ Words of a song	**Lyrics**
✠ Words that are written on or cut into a surface	**Inscription**
✠ Worst or lowest points of something	**Nadir**
✠ Writings that are about facts or real events	**Non-fiction**
✠ Written accounts in which someone (such as a famous performer or politician) describes past experiences	**Memoirs**
✠ Written constitutions or description of organisations' functions	**Charter**
✠ Written laws that are formally created by a government	**Statute**
✠ Written or spoken expressions of great enthusiasm, praise, etc	**Rhapsody**
✠ Written or spoken statements in which you say that you have done something wrong or committed a crime	**Confession**
✠ Written statements that describe the policies, goals, and opinions of a person or group	**Manifesto**
✠ Written, printed, or typed copy of words that have been spoken	**Transcript**

- Young person in the process of developing from a child into an adult **Adolescent**
- Young child who is just learning to walk **Toddler**
- Young person who behaves badly and who does dangerous, foolish, or illegal things **Tearaway**
- Young person who is taught and helped by someone who has a lot of knowledge and experience **Protégé**
- Young person who is unusually talented in some way **Prodigy**
- Young woman who is not married **Damsel**

Words in Categories

A: Arts and Crafts

- Art made on a public surface, such as a building or a street sign, that is not owned by the artist — **Graffiti**
- Art of designing and constructing buildings — **Architecture**
- Art of photographing and lighting films, also the style or genre of a movie or motion picture — **Cinematography**
- Artwork on floor made with an inlay of wood of different colours — **Parquet**
- Artwork using various materials — **Collage**
- Clay objects hardened by heat — **Pottery**
- Covering a surface with a thin layer of gold — **Gild (v)**
- Cutting of designs into hard surface — **Engraving**
- Decorating surfaces with raised ornamentation — **Embossing**
- Delicate fabrics made of yarn ; gold or silver ornamental braid — **Lace**
- Engraved designing on a plate surface — **Intaglio**
- Exposing human vices and follies to ridicule or scorn — **Satire**
- Giving movement to something ; the process of making moving cartoons or films that use cartoon imagery — **Animation**
- Hand-dyed patterns on fabrics — **Batik**
- Hard, brown-red unglazed earthenware — **Terra cotta**
- Heavy decorative cloth hung on a wall — **Tapestry**
- Highly decorative hand-writing — **Calligraphy**
- Ideal or perfect society ; utopias are imagined communities where everyone lives in perfect peace and harmony — **Utopia**

✠ Images or stories that refer to a related or overarching concepts such as good or evil	**Allegory**
✠ Inlaid works made from small pieces of coloured wood or other materials, used for the decoration of furniture	**Marquetry**
✠ Japanese art of arranging flowers in artistic designs	**Ikebana**
✠ Japanese decorative art of creating shapes by folding paper	**Origami**
✠ Knitting with a hooked needle	**Crocheting**
✠ Literally, a vocabulary; a collection of terms or characteristics used in a particular profession, subject, or style	**Lexicon**
✠ Making designs on a metal plate or glass by the corrosive action of acid	**Etching**
✠ Means of categorising works of art based on style, form, and subject matter	**Genre**
✠ Name, symbol or a trademark	**Logo**
✠ Object produced or shaped by human craft	**Artifact**
✠ Ornamental work of delicate, intricate design with thin metal wire	**Filigree**
✠ Outline that appears dark against a light background or a dark shape seen against a light surface	**Silhouette**
✠ Person who is responsible for the collection, care, research, and exhibition of art or artifacts	**Curator**
✠ Photographs of inanimate objects	**Still-life**
✠ Pictures or patterns produced by arranging together small pieces of stone , tile, glass, etc	**Mosaics**
✠ Pieces of art that are made by carving or molding clay, stone, metal, etc	**Sculpture**
✠ Pleasing in appearance and to the senses	**Aesthetic**
✠ Recurrent or dominant themes in a work of visual or literary art	**Motif**

- Relationships between disparate visual and verbal sources where one kind of object, idea or image is used in place of another to suggest a likeness or analogy between them — **Metaphor**
- Representation of a person or thing that exaggerates his/her/its most striking or characteristic features — **Caricature**
- Screen printings on silks — **Serigraphy**
- Single pictorial composition made by juxtaposing many pictures or designs — **Montage**
- Style, arrangement, or appearance of printed letters on a page — **Typography**
- Symbols and images that have a particular meaning, either learned or universal — **Iconography**
- Thin layers of finely grained wood over another surface — **Veneer**
- Three-dimensional photography using split laser beam — **Holography**

B : *Body Systems*

- Connected with glands that put hormones and other products directly into the blood — **Endocrine**
- Connected with the body's nerves and often affecting you mentally or emotionally — **Nervous**
- Connected with the muscles — **Muscular**
- Connected with the skeleton of a person or an animal — **Skeletal**
- Connected with urine or the parts of the body through which it passes — **Urinary**
- Of or relating to both the stomach and the intestines — **Gastrointestinal**
- Of or relating to breathing or the organs of the body that are used in breathing — **Respiratory**
- Of or relating to the heart and blood vessels — **Cardiovascular**

✠ Related to the tough outer protective layer, especially that of an animal or plant	**Integumentary**
✠ Relating to lymph or its secretion	**Lymphatic**
✠ Relating to or involved in the production of babies, young animals, or new plants	**Reproductive**
✠ The tough outer protective layer, especially that of an animal or plant	**Sensory**

C : *Crime and Punishment*

✠ A threatened or attempted physical attack by someone who appears to be able to cause bodily harm if not stopped	**Assault**
✠ A trial period during which your character and abilities are tested to see whether you are suitable for work or for the membership	**Probation**
✠ An assault with intent to rob	**Mugging**
✠ Confinement during wartime ; the act of confining someone in a prison (or as if in a prison) ; placing private property in the custody of an officer of the law	**Internment**
✠ Dealing or trading in something illegal	**Trafficking**
✠ Entering a building unlawfully with an intent to commit a felony or to steal valuable property	**Burglary**
✠ Entering someone's land or property without permission	**Trespassing**
✠ Extortion of money by threats to divulge discrediting informations	**Blackmail**
✠ Homicide without malice aforethought	**Manslaughter**
✠ Illegally hunting or catching (game or fish) on land that is not one's own or in contravention of official protection	**Poaching**
✠ Larceny by threat of violence ; plundering during riots or in wartime	**Robbery**
✠ Malicious burning to destroy property	**Arson**

✠ Murder of a public figure by a surprise attack ; an attack intended to ruin someone's reputation	**Assassination**
✠ Putting a condemned person to death	**Capital punishment**
✠ Secretly importing prohibited goods or the goods on which duty is due	**Smuggling**
✠ Something intended to deceive ; deliberate trickery intended to gain an advantage	**Fraud**
✠ Systematic killing of a racial or a cultural group	**Genocide**
✠ The act of stealing goods that are on display in a store	**Shoplifting**
✠ The crime of betraying one's country, especially by attempting to kill or overthrow the sovereign or government	**Treason**
✠ The criminal falsification by making or altering an instrument with intent to defraud ; a copy that is represented as the original	**Forgery**
✠ The expulsion of someone (such as a tenant) from the possession of land by the process of law	**Eviction**
✠ The fraudulent appropriation of funds or property entrusted to your care but actually owned by someone else	**Embezzlement**
✠ The killing of a human being by another human being	**Homicide**
✠ The offence of marrying someone else while you have a living spouse from whom you haven't taken a valid divorce	**Bigamy**
✠ The offence of wilfully telling an untruth or making a misrepresentation under oath	**Perjury**
✠ The practice of offering something (usually money) in order to gain an illicit advantage	**Bribery**
✠ The robbery of a traveller or vehicle in transit or seizing control of a vehicle by the use of force	**Hijacking**
✠ The systematic use of spies to get military or political secrets	**Espionage**

- ✠ The unofficial or unauthorised use of violence and intimidation in the pursuit of political aims **Terrorism**
- ✠ The wilful destruction of or damage to public or private property **Vandalism**
- ✠ Word falsely spoken that damages the reputation of another; an abusive attack on a person's character or good name **Slander**

D : *Natural Disasters*

- ✠ A long period of time during which there is very little or no rain **Drought**
- ✠ A long, high sea wave caused by an earthquake or other disturbance **Tsunami**
- ✠ A prolonged period of abnormally hot weather **Heatwave**
- ✠ A severe snowstorm that goes on for a long time **Blizzard**
- ✠ A situation in which many people do not have enough food to eat **Famine**
- ✠ A storm during which small balls of ice fall from the sky **Hailstorm**
- ✠ A storm with thunder and lightning and usually very heavy rain **Thunderstorm**
- ✠ A very bad weather with strong winds and rain, and often thunder and lightning **Storm**
- ✠ A violent and destructive storm in which powerful winds move around a central point **Tornadoe**
- ✠ An occurrence in which a disease spreads very quickly and affects a large number of people **Epidemic**
- ✠ Flashes of light that are produced in the sky during a storm **Lightning**
- ✠ The extremely large, powerful, and destructive storms with very high winds that turn around an area of low pressure **Cyclones**
- ✠ The extremely large, powerful, and destructive storms with very strong winds **Hurricanes**

- The extremely large, powerful, and destructive storms **Typhoons**
- The fire in a wild area (such as a forest) that is not controlled and that can burn a large area very quickly **Wildfire**
- The fire in scrub or a forest, especially one that spreads rapidly **Bushfire**
- The large amount of snow and ice or of dirt and rocks that slides suddenly down the side of a mountain **Avalanches**
- The large amount of water covering an area of land that is usually dry **Floods**
- The large mass of rocks and Earth that suddenly and quickly moves down the side of a mountain or hill **Landslide**
- The large mass of wet Earth that suddenly and quickly moves down the side of a mountain or hill **Mudslides**
- Shaking of a part of the Earth's surface that often causes great damage **Earthquake**

E : *Types of Government*

- A centralised government **Endarchy**
- A personal rule; self-rule **Idiocracy**
- An opposition to government; anarchy **Antarchy**
- The government based on legal system; rule of law **Nomocracy**
- The government by a body of foreigners **Xenocracy**
- The government by a foreign ruler **Heterarchy**
- The government by an absolute ruler **Autarchy**
- The government by an ethnic group or race **Ethnocracy**
- The government by civil servants **Bureaucracy**
- The government by corporate bureaucrats **Corpocracy**
- The government by despots or tyrants **Despotocracy**
- The government by judges **Kritarchy**

✠ The government by many rulers	**Polycracy**
✠ The government by men or fathers	**Patriarchy**
✠ The government by mobs or crowds	**Mobocracy**
✠ The government by mobs	**Ochlocracy**
✠ The government by money	**Argentocracy**
✠ The government by new or inexperienced rulers	**Neocracy**
✠ The government by none	**Anarchy, Acracy**
✠ The government by one individual	**Autocracy, Monarchy**
✠ The government by physical force	**Chirocracy**
✠ The government by priests or by religious law	**Theocracy**
✠ The government by saints or holy persons	**Hagiarchy**
✠ The government by simple majority	**Arithmocracy**
✠ The government by technical experts	**Technocracy**
✠ The government by the best	**Aristarchy**
✠ The government by the few	**Oligarchy**
✠ The government by the meritorious	**Meritocracy**
✠ The government by the military	**Hoplarchy**
✠ The government by the nobility	**Aristocracy**
✠ The government by the people	**Democracy**
✠ The government by the people; popular government	**Demarchy**
✠ The government by the wealthy	**Plutocracy**
✠ The government by two people	**Diarchy, Duarchy**
✠ The government by white people	**Albocracy**
✠ The government by women or mothers	**Matriarchy**
✠ The government in an unstructured fashion; an unstructured organisation	**Adhocracy**
✠ The rule by a God or Gods; body of divine rulers	**Thearchy**

F : Isms

✠ A belief in all religions	**Omnism**
✠ A belief in ghosts	**Eidolism**
✠ A belief in maintaining political and social traditions	**Conservatism**
✠ A belief in multiple deities	**Polytheism**
✠ A belief in only one God	**Monotheism**
✠ A belief in sentimental feeling in artistic expression	**Romanticism**
✠ A belief that humans ought to be equal in rights and privileges	**Egalitarianism**
✠ A belief that matter is the only extant substance	**Materialism**
✠ A belief that nothing is real except the soul or spirit	**Spiritualism**
✠ A belief that our experiences of the world consist of ideas	**Idealism**
✠ A belief that pleasure is the highest good	**Hedonism**
✠ A belief that reality consists of several kinds or entities	**Pluralism**
✠ A belief that reason is the fundamental source of knowledge	**Rationalism**
✠ A belief that there is no God	**Atheism**
✠ A doctrine emphasising practical value of philosophy	**Pragmatism**
✠ A doctrine of centralised state control of wealth and property	**Socialism**
✠ A doctrine of communal control of means of production	**Collectivism**
✠ A doctrine of social change and tolerance	**Liberalism**
✠ A doctrine that all governments should be abolished	**Anarchism**

- ✠ A doctrine that events are fixed and humans are powerless — **Fatalism**
- ✠ A doctrine that objects of cognition are real — **Realism**
- ✠ A doctrine that private ownership and free markets should govern economies — **Capitalism**
- ✠ A doctrine that the highest moral obligation is to improve human welfare — **Humanitarianism**
- ✠ A doctrine that the pursuit of self-interest is the highest good — **Egoism**
- ✠ A doctrine that there is only one kind of existence — **Henism**
- ✠ A doctrine that we live in the best of all possible worlds — **Optimism**
- ✠ The belief that matter has existed eternally — **Eternalism**
- ✠ The denial of all reality; extreme scepticism — **Nihilism**

G : *Law*

- ✠ The act of keeping someone in a prison or similar place — **Detention**
- ✠ The act or instance of waiving a right or claim — **Waiver**
- ✠ The amount of money given to a court to allow a prisoner to leave jail and return later for a trial — **Bail**
- ✠ Based on the first impression; accepted as correct until proved otherwise — **Prima facie**
- ✠ A charge (a public official) with a crime done while in office — **Impeachment**
- ✠ A condition of being bankrupt ; a condition of financial failure caused by not having the money that you need to pay your debts — **Bankruptcy**
- ✠ A crime that is not very serious ; a crime that is less serious than a felony — **Misdemeanor**

- ✠ A document issued by a legal or government official authorising the police or another body to make an arrest, search premises, or carry out some other action relating to the administration of justice — **Warrant**
- ✠ An explanation or warning that should be remembered when you are doing or thinking about something — **Caveat**
- ✠ A form of written command in the name of a court or other legal authority to act, or abstain from acting, in a particular way — **Writ**
- ✠ A formal written request to have a legal case decided by a court — **Petition**
- ✠ The group of people who are members of the public and are chosen to make a decision in a legal case — **Jury**
- ✠ An impartial adviser to a court of law in a particular case — **Amicus curiae**
- ✠ Instead of something else — **In lieu**
- ✠ A judicial writ issued as a command to an inferior court or ordering a person to perform a public or statutory duty — **Mandamus**
- ✠ A law or an order that stops something from being used or done — **Prohibition**
- ✠ Laws or regulations made by a city, town or the government — **Ordinance**
- ✠ A lawyer in Britain who assists people in legal matters and who can represent people in lower courts of law — **Solicitor**
- ✠ A lawyer who represents the side in a court case that accuses a person of a crime and who tries to prove that the person is guilty — **Prosecutor**
- ✠ A list of the legal cases that will be tried in a court of law — **Docket**

✠ To make something the subject of a lawsuit ; to cause a case, an issue, etc to be decided and settled in a court of law	**Litigation**
✠ The money that a court orders someone to pay regularly to a former wife or husband after a divorce	**Alimony**
✠ Not valid or legally binding	**Void**
✠ An official order given by a person with power or by a government	**Decree**
✠ An official written statement charging a person with a crime	**Indictment**
✠ On his own motion	**Suo Motu**
✠ One of the formal, usually written statements made by the two sides of a legal case in a court of law	**Pleadings**
✠ An order for the intervening period; provisional order	**Interim Order**
✠ The permission given to a prisoner to leave prison before the end of a sentence usually as a reward for behaving well	**Parole**
✠ Persons giving sworn testimony to a court of law or the police	**Witness**
✠ A person who commits a crime	**Offender**
✠ A person who gives a response or answer to a question that is asked especially as part of a survey	**Respondent**
✠ A person who is being sued or accused of a crime in a court of law	**Defendant**
✠ A person who sues another person or accuses another person of a crime in a court of law	**Plaintiff**
✠ The person, typically a lawyer, appointed to act for another in business or legal matters	**Attorney**
✠ The places where a judge sits in a court of law	**Bench**
✠ The power or right to make judgments about the law, to arrest and punish criminals, etc	**Jurisdiction**

✠ The process of settling an argument or disagreement in which the people or groups on both sides present their opinions and ideas to a third person or group	**Arbitration**
✠ To produce satisfactory grounds for application of (or exemption from) a procedure or penalty	**Show Cause**
✠ Responsible for committing a crime or doing something bad or wrong	**Guilty**
✠ The right or capacity to bring an action or to appear in a court	**Locus Standi**
✠ To say in a will that your property will be given to a person or organisation after you die	**Bequeath**
✠ A serious crime (such as murder or rape)	**Felony**
✠ To show, prove, or state that something is true or real	**Attestation**
✠ A situation or period of time in which a person who has committed a crime is allowed to stay out of prison if that person behaves well and does not commit another crime, etc	**Probation**
✠ Something (such as the payment of money) for which a person or business is legally responsible	**Liability**
✠ Something that is done or given freely rather than because it is required by a law	**Ex gratia**
✠ To state the charges against someone who is accused of a crime in a formal procedure before a judge	**Arraignment**
✠ The statement in which a person who has been accused of a crime says in court that he or she is guilty or not guilty of the crime	**Plea**
✠ A summary of the facts and legal points in a case given to a barrister to argue in court	**Brief**
✠ A thing that has already happened or been decided before those affected hear about it, leaving them with no option but to accept it	**Fait accompli**

- ✠ Under a judicial consideration and therefore prohibited from public discussion elsewhere — **Sub judice**
- ✠ An unreasonable delay in asserting a claim, which may result in its dismissal — **Laches**
- ✠ To use the power of the law to take and keep someone (such as a criminal) — **Arrest**
- ✠ Usually a rude or angry reply to something written or said — **Rejoinder**
- ✠ Who becomes involved in a lawsuit as a third party — **Intervenor**
- ✠ A writ or legal action requiring a person to show by what warrant an office or franchise is held, claimed, or exercised — **Quo warranto**
- ✠ A writ requiring a person under arrest to be brought before a judge or into court, especially to secure the person's release unless lawful grounds are shown for their detention — **Habeas Corpus**
- ✠ A written law that is formally created by a government — **Statute**
- ✠ A written or spoken statement in which you say that you have done something wrong or committed a crime — **Confession**
- ✠ A written report which is signed by a person who promises that the information is true — **Affidavit**

H : *Literary Terms*

- ✠ An act of referring to something by the name of something else that is closely connected with it — **Metonymy**
- ✠ An agreement or compatibility between opinions or actions — **Consonance**
- ✠ An apparition or double of a living person — **Doppelganger**
- ✠ Being a warning or indication of a future event — **Foreshadowing**
- ✠ The change in the position, order, or relationship of things so that they are the opposite of what they had been — **Inversion**

- Clearness of a person's speech **Diction**
- A combination of words that have opposite or very different meanings **Oxymoron**
- A compound expression in Old English and Old Norse poetry with metaphorical meaning **Kennings**
- An exact opposite of something or someone **Antithesis**
- The figure of speech in which a part is made to represent the whole or *vice versa* **Synecdoche**
- The figure of speech in which a word is applied to two others of which it grammatically suits only one **Syllepsis**
- The final section or speech after the main part of a book, play, or musical composition **Epilogue**
- The formation of a word from a sound associated with what is named **Onomatopoeia**
- Giving more information about (something), such as a statement **Amplification**
- The group of lines in a poem **Stanza**
- A humorous way of using a word or phrase so that more than one meaning is suggested **Puns**
- An idea or a quality that a word makes you think about in addition to its meaning **Connotation**
- Introduction to a book, play, etc **Prologue**
- An inversion of the normal order of words, especially for the sake of emphasis **Hyperbaton**
- An inversion of the usual order of words or clauses **Anastrophe**
- Language that describes something as better or worse than it really is **Hyperbole**
- A literal or primary meaning of a word, in contrast to the feelings or ideas that the word suggests **Denotation**
- A main subject that is being discussed or described in a piece of writing, a movie, etc **Theme**

✠ A mild or pleasant word or phrase that is used instead of one that is unpleasant or offensive	**Euphemism**
✠ A mistaken use of a word in place of a similar-sounding one, often with an amusing effect	**Malapropism**
✠ A novel dealing with one person's formative years or spiritual education	**Bildungsroman**
✠ An omission or absence of a conjunction between parts of a sentence	**Asyndeton**
✠ One of two or more words or phrases that ends in the same sounds	**Rhyme**
✠ An opponent or enemy that is very difficult to defeat	**Nemesis**
✠ The part of a story or movie that describes or shows something that happened in the past	**Flashback**
✠ A pause near the middle of a line	**Caesura**
✠ A perfect example of something	**Archetype**
✠ A person who has a lot of a particular quality and who is the perfect example of someone who has that quality	**Personification**
✠ A phrase that uses the words *like* or *as* to describe someone or something by comparing it with someone or something else that is similar	**Simile**
✠ Different things together in order to create an interesting effect or to show how they are the same or different	**Juxtapose**
✠ A practice of foretelling the future by interpreting a randomly chosen passage from a book, especially the Bible	**Bibliomancy**
✠ The production of a sense impression relating to one sense or part of the body by stimulation of another sense or part of the body	**Synesthesia**
✠ The quality of a person's voice	**Tone**
✠ The quality of being pleasing to the ear	**Euphony**

✠ The quality of seeming real	**Verisimilitude**
✠ The regular, repeated pattern of sounds or movements	**Rhythm**
✠ The rhetorical or literary figure in which words, grammatical constructions, or concepts are repeated in reverse order	**Chiasmus**
✠ The short phrase that expresses a true or wise idea	**Aphorism**
✠ The short story that teaches a moral or spiritual lesson	**Parable**
✠ The short story that usually is about animals and that is intended to teach a lesson	**Fable**
✠ Something (such as a situation) that is made up of two opposite things and that seems impossible but is actually true or possible	**Paradox**
✠ Something (such as an important idea or subject) that is repeated throughout a book, story, etc	**Motif**
✠ A statement that makes something seem smaller, less important, etc, than it really is	**Understatement**
✠ A statement that refers to something without mentioning it directly	**Allusion**
✠ A story in which the characters and events are symbols that stand for ideas about human life or for a political or historical situation	**Allegory**
✠ A story in which the characters and events are symbols that stand for ideas about human life or for a political or historical situation	**Analogy**
✠ A thing regarded as representative or symbolic of something else	**Metaphor**
✠ A try to be like (someone or something you admire)	**Emulation**
✠ An unexpected power or event saving a seemingly hopeless situation	**Deus ex Machina**
✠ The unpleasant loud sounds	**Cacophony**

- ✠ The use of indirect and circumlocutory speech or writing **Periphrasis**
- ✠ The use of many words to say something that could be said more clearly and directly by using fewer words **Circumlocution**
- ✠ The use of words that begin with the same sound near one another **Alliteration**
- ✠ The use of words that have the same or very similar vowel sounds near one another **Assonance**
- ✠ The use of words that mean the opposite of what you really think especially in order to be funny **Irony**
- ✠ A verbal error in which a speaker accidentally transposes the initial sounds or letters of two or more words, often to humorous effect **Spoonerism**
- ✠ A very bad event that causes great sadness and often involves someone's death **Tragedy**
- ✠ A way in which words are put together to form phrases, clauses, or sentences **Syntax**
- ✠ A way of using humour to show that someone or something is foolish, weak, bad, etc. **Satire**
- ✠ A word or phrase made by changing the order of the letters in another word or phrase **Anagram**
- ✠ A word or phrase that describes a person or thing **Epithet**
- ✠ A writing in which words are arranged in a rhythmic pattern **Verse**

I : *Manias*

- ✠ An abnormal belief that one is divinely inspired **Entheomania**
- ✠ An abnormal desire to return to familiar places **Ostomania**
- ✠ An abnormal sexual interest **Aphrodisiomania**
- ✠ An addiction to poisonous substances (e.g. drugs) **Toxicomania**
- ✠ An addiction to smoking tobacco products **Capnomania**
- ✠ An addiction to the Internet **Netomania**

✠ Alcoholism; an excessive desire to drink alcoholic beverages	**Alcoholomania**
✠ A compulsion to collect and possess books	**Bibliomania**
✠ A compulsion to commit murder	**Homicidomania**
✠ A compulsion to eat	**Oreximania**
✠ A compulsion to steal	**Kleptomania**
✠ A compulsion to think	**Phronemomania**
✠ A compulsion to travel	**Hodomania**
✠ A compulsion to wander	**Ecdemomania**
✠ A compulsion to war	**Polemomania**
✠ A compulsive or abnormal desire to talk excessively	**Lalomania**
✠ A compulsive pursuit of pleasure	**Hedonomania**
✠ A craze for technology	**Technomania**
✠ A delusion that one is beautiful	**Callomania**
✠ A delusional belief that one is of great importance	**Megalomania**
✠ An excessive fondness for and preoccupation with animals	**Zoomania**
✠ An excessive fondness for cats	**Ailuromania**
✠ An excessive interest in music	**Melomania**
✠ An excessive or abnormal desire for wealth	**Plutomania**
✠ An excessive tendency towards materialism	**Hylomania**
✠ The hatred of everything	**Misomania**
✠ The homicidal insanity	**Androphonomania**
✠ In females, abnormally strong desire to have a child	**Nepiomania**
✠ An insatiable urge to hold public office	**Empleomania**
✠ An intense desire to be alone or out in the open	**Agromania**
✠ An intense nervous depression	**Lypemania**
✠ An irrational craving for water	**Hydromania**
✠ An irrational predilection for lying	**Pseudomania**

✠ A mania for sainthood	**Hagiomania**
✠ A morbid and insatiable craving for alcohol	**Dipsomania**
✠ An obsession with a particular food	**Opsomania**
✠ An obsession with children	**Pedomania**
✠ An obsession with crowds	**Ochlomania**
✠ An obsession with food and eating	**Phagomania**
✠ An obsession with food	**Sitiomania**
✠ An obsession with home	**Oikomania**
✠ An obsession with imagined disease	**Nosomania**
✠ An obsession with killing	**Dacnomania**
✠ An obsession with money	**Chrematomania**
✠ An obsession with night	**Noctimania**
✠ An obsession with time	**Chronomania**
✠ An obsession with writing	**Scribomania**
✠ An obsessional belief that one has sinned	**Enosimania**
✠ An obsessional preoccupation with cleanliness, washing or bathing	**Ablutomania**
✠ An obsessive devotion to one's own race, people or ancestry	**Ethnomania**
✠ An obsessive interest in foreigners or for things foreign	**Xenomania**
✠ An obsessive need to work	**Ergasiomania**
✠ An obsessive preoccupation with numbers	**Arithmomania**
✠ An obsessive preoccupation with the self	**Egomania**
✠ A religious insanity	**Sebastomania**
✠ A sexual craving for women	**Gynaecomania**
✠ A strong desire for freedom	**Eleutheromania**
✠ An uncontrollable impulse to wander or travel	**Dromomania**

J : Phobias

✠ The fear of accidents	**Dystychiphobia**
✠ The fear of aeroplanes/ flying	**Aerophobia**
✠ The fear of animals	**Zoophobia**
✠ The fear of baldness	**Phalacrophobia**
✠ The fear of blood	**Haemophobia, Haematophobia**
✠ The fear of confined spaces	**Claustrophobia**
✠ The fear of crossing streets	**Dromophobia**
✠ The fear of crowds	**Demophobia**
✠ The fear of dark	**Nyctophobia, Lygophobia**
✠ The fear of death/dead bodies	**Necrophobia, Thanatophobia**
✠ The fear of dentists	**Dentophobia**
✠ The fear of depths/deep places	**Bathophobia**
✠ The fear of dogs	**Cynophobia**
✠ The fear of electricity	**Electrophobia**
✠ The fear of fire	**Pyrophobia**
✠ The fear of germs	**Verminophobia**
✠ The fear of ghosts	**Phasmophobia**
✠ The fear of heights	**Acrophobia**
✠ The fear of hospitals	**Nosocomephobia**
✠ The fear of illness	**Pathophobia**
✠ The fear of injections	**Trypanophobia**
✠ The fear of lightning	**Astrapophobia**
✠ The fear of loneliness	**Monophobia**
✠ The fear of machines	**Mechanophobia**
✠ The fear of madness/insanity	**Maniaphobia**
✠ The fear of new things	**Neophobia**

✠ The fear of old age	**Gerascophobia**
✠ The fear of open spaces/going out in public	**Agoraphobia**
✠ The fear of outer space	**Spacephobia**
✠ The fear of pain	**Algophobia**
✠ The fear of sharks	**Galeophobia**
✠ The fear of snakes	**Ophidiophobia**
✠ The fear of society or people in general	**Sociophobia**
✠ The fear of speaking/public speaking	**Lalophobia, Glossophobia**
✠ The fear of surgery	**Tomophobia**
✠ The fear of vehicles	**Ochophobia**
✠ The fear of voids or empty spaces	**Kenophobia**
✠ The fear of water	**Hydrophobia**

PREVIOUS YEARS' QUESTIONS

PREVIOUS YEARS' QUESTIONS

SET 1

Direction *In the following questions out of the four alternatives, select the one which is the best substitute of the phrase.*

1. An uneducated person **[SSC Multitasking Staff 2017]**
(a) joker (b) clown
(c) instructor (d) illiterate

2. A person learning a trade under someone **[SSC MTS 2017]**
(a) assistant (b) secretary (c) clerk (d) apprentice

3. Complete with regard to every detail **[SSC CGL 2017]**
(a) thorough (b) lackadaisical (c) lax (d) cursory

4. Line at which earth and sky or sea seem to meet **[SSC CAP 2017]**
(a) nadir (b) zenith (c) horizon (d) trivet

5. A place for fish or water plant **[SSC CAP 2017]**
(a) aviary (b) apiary (c) herbarium (d) aquarium

6. To sweep over something so as to surround it completely **[SSC CHSL 2017]**
(a) engulf (b) imbibe (c) drown (d) plunge

7. To take someone somewhere suddenly and quickly **[SSC CHSL 2017]**
(a) rush (b) whisk (c) fly (d) flit

8. A hollow object used to contain something **[SSC CHSL 2017]**
(a) platter (b) solver (c) plate (d) receptacle

9. What do we call a lifeless object **[SSC CAP 2017]**
(a) amateur (b) inanimate (c) alien (d) amnesty

10. A house where children with no parents are taken care of **[SSC Multitasking Staff 2017]**
(a) creche (b) hospital (c) nursery (d) orphanage

11. A person who escapes from hard realities **[Chhattisgarh Revenue Inspector 2017]**
(a) escapist (b) rapist (c) polyglot (d) benefactor

12. That which is unlawful **[SSC Multitasking Staff 2017]**
(a) legal (b) court (c) bail (d) illicit

13. Animal that can live on land and in water **[SSC CGL 2017]**
(a) anthropoid (b) aquatic (c) amphibian (d) marsupial

14. A hater of women **[SSC CGL 2017]**
(a) monarchist (b) misanthrope (c) philanderer (d) misogynist

15. A state where there is no effective government **[SSC CGL 2017]**
(a) secular (b) democracy (c) governance (d) anarchy

16. A person who opposes war or use of military force **[SSC CGL 2017]**
(a) narcissist (b) fatalist (c) pacifist (d) fascist

17. Substance used in surgery to produce unconsciousness **[SSC CGL 2017]**
(a) antiseptic (b) antidote (c) anesthetic (d) cocaine

18. Master of ceremonies **[SSC CGL 2017]**
(a) ceremonist (b) compere (c) organiser (d) manager

19. A remedy for all diseases **[SSC LDC 2017, SSC CAPFs SI 2015, ASI 2015, SSC CGL 2011]**
(a) tonic (b) nectar (c) panacea (d) elixir

20. The act of killing a whole group of people specially a whole race **[SSC CGL 2017]**
(a) patricide (b) genocide (c) parricide (d) matricide

21. Made or done without previous preparation **[SSC Multitasking Staff 2017]**
(a) immediate (b) impromptu (c) urgent (d) prompt

22. A court or open space usually rectangular and enclosed by a building **[Chhattisgarh Revenue Inspector 2017]**
(a) quadragenarian (b) quadrilateral (c) quadrangle (d) quadruped

23. Bringing about gentle and painless death from incurable disease **[SSC CGL 2017]**
(a) euthanasia (b) sty (c) canicide (d) suicide

24. The study of birds is known as **[SSC CGL 2017]**
(a) ornithology (b) zoology (c) biology (d) anatomy

25. The belief that everyone is equal and should have the same rights and opportunities **[SSC CGL 2017]**
(a) altruistic (b) egoistic (c) egalitarian (d) octogenarian

26. Irresistible craving for alcoholic drink **[SSC CGL 2017]**
(a) pyromania (b) dipsomania (c) megalomania (d) kleptomania

27. One who lives on fish **[Uttarakhand PSC 2017]**
(a) carnivorous (b) baccivorous (c) aurivorous (d) piscivorous

28. A study of the origin and history of words **[Uttarakhand PSC 2017]**
(a) anthropology (b) morphology
(c) linguistics (d) etymology

Previous Years' Questions

29. Printed notice of somebody's death **[SSC CGL 2016]**
(a) mourning (b) obituary (c) condolence (d) commiseration

30. A loud harsh piercing cry **[SSC CGL 2016]**
(a) noise (b) howl (c) screech (d) cry

31. That which can not be believed **[SSC CGL 2016]**
(a) awesome (b) incredible (c) credible (d) ineffective

32. One who does or studies without seriousness **[SSC PO & SSI Online 2016]**
(a) dilettante (b) diligent (c) deliberate (d) distracted

33. Sudden involuntary muscular contraction **[SSC CGL Tier-l 2016]**
(a) sprain (b) spasm (c) spam (d) span

34. A group of islands **[SSC CGL Tier-I 2016]**
(a) islet (b) archipelago (c) reef (d) atoll

35. Insatiable desire for wealth **[SSC CGL 2016]**
(a) selfish (b) avarice (c) egoist (d) generosity

36. Constant effort to achieve something **[SSC CAPFs SI, ASI 2016]**
(a) patience (b) vigour (c) enthusiasm (d) perseverance

37. A place where birds are kept **[SSC SOA 2007]**
(a) aquarium (b) den (c) aviary (d) sanctuary

38. Responsible according to law **[SSC CAPF's 2016]**
(a) eligible (b) illegitimate (c) legalised (d) liable

39. Opposed to great or sudden change **[SSC CAPF's 2016]**
(a) conservative (b) revolutionary (c) evolutionary (d) static

40. Place given to soldiers to live in **[SSC CGL Tier-I 2016]**
(a) barracks (b) trench (c) garage (d) quay

41. One who pretends to be what he is not **[SSC CGL 2016]**
(a) hypocrite (b) pessimist (c) optimist (d) infallible

42. An action or event that happens before another important one and forms an introduction to it **[SSC CGL Tier-I 2016]**
(a) foreword (b) predecessor (c) prefix (d) prelude

43. A computer printout sent out by a bank regarding debits and credits in your account **[SSC CGL 2016]**
(a) bank draft (b) statement (c) over-draft (d) payee

44. Refresh and revive **[SSC CGL 2016]**
(a) invigorate (b) investigate (c) invalidate (d) invigilate

45. Strange in appearance **[SSC CPO 2016]**
(a) bizarre (b) rustic
(c) geriatric (d) decreipt

46. Enigmatic person **[SSC CPO 2016]**
(a) unique (b) unstable (c) stable (d) unknownable

47. A place where coins are made **[SSC CGL 2016]**
(a) mint (b) factory (c) cannery (d) monetary

48. Those who pass through this gate without permission **[SSC CPO 2016]**
(a) passersby (b) tresspassers (c) culprits (d) absconders

49. To send someone back to his or her own country **[SSC CPO 2016]**
(a) extirpate (b) repatriate (c) expropriate (d) exile

50. A person between 90 and 100 years old **[SSC CPO 2016]**
(a) septugenarian (b) nonagenarian
(c) centenarian (d) octogenarian

ANSWERS

1 *(d)*	**2** *(d)*	**3** *(a)*	**4** *(c)*	**5** *(d)*	**6** *(a)*	**7** *(b)*	**8** *(d)*	**9** *(c)*	**10** *(d)*
11 *(a)*	**12** *(d)*	**13** *(c)*	**14** *(d)*	**15** *(d)*	**16** *(c)*	**17** *(c)*	**18** *(b)*	**19** *(c)*	**20** *(b)*
21 *(b)*	**22** *(c)*	**23** *(a)*	**24** *(a)*	**25** *(c)*	**26** *(b)*	**27** *(d)*	**28** *(d)*	**29** *(b)*	**30** *(c)*
31 *(b)*	**32** *(a)*	**33** *(b)*	**34** *(b)*	**35** *(b)*	**36** *(d)*	**37** *(b)*	**38** *(d)*	**39** *(a)*	**40** *(a)*
41 *(a)*	**42** *(d)*	**43** *(b)*	**44** *(a)*	**45** *(a)*	**46** *(d)*	**47** *(a)*	**48** *(b)*	**49** *(b)*	**50** *(b)*

SET 2

Direction *In the following questions out of the four alternatives, select the one which is the best substitute of the phrase.*

1. A large body of people playing various musical instruments **[SSC CGL 2016]**
(a) melody (b) harmony (c) elocution (d) orchestra

2. An animal that lives in groups **[SSC CGL 2016]**
(a) hoard (b) fastidious (c) gullible (d) gregarious

3. Hard working and diligent **[SSC CGL 2016]**
(a) seditious (b) sedate (c) sedulous (d) scheming

4. The act of showing disrespect towards sacred things **[SSC CGL 2016]**
(a) congregation (b) etymology
(c) panjandrum (d) blasphemy

5. Favouritism shown by a person in power to his relatives **[SSC CGL 2016]**
(a) formalism (b) red - tapism (c) nepotism (d) bureaucracy

6. Committing murder in revenge **[SSC CGL 2016]**
(a) massacre (b) vendetta (c) homicide (d) regicide

Previous Years' Questions

7. The thing that can be easily broken **[SSC CGL 2016]**
(a) amorphous (b) brittle (c) subtle (d) solid

8. An unimportant person **[SSC CGL 2016]**
(a) nonagenarian (b) nonentity (c) nonpareil (d) nonconformist

9. Suitable or intended only for young persons **[SSC CGL 2016]**
(a) youthful (b) puerile (c) adolescent (d) juvenile

10. Money given to agent on sales **[SSC CGL 2016]**
(a) help (b) commission (c) assignment (d) endeavour

11. Person believing in one marriage **[SSC CGL 2016]**
(a) polygamist (b) misogynist (c) monogamist (d) philanthropist

12. A system of government in which only one political party is allowed to function **[SSC CGL 2016]**
(a) oligarchy (b) dictatorship (c) totalitarianism (d) theocracy

13. Art of designing or writing on wax **[SSC CGL Tier-I 2016]**
(a) cartography (b) cerography (c) psephology (d) etymology

14. A round about way of expression **[SSC CGL 2016]**
(a) verbosity (b) talkativeness (c) circumlocution (d) loquacious

15. Belong to the same period **[SSC CGL 2016]**
(a) comrades (b) contemporaries
(c) compromises (d) renegades

16. One who listens secretly to private conversation **[SSC CGL 2016]**
(a) eavesdropper (b) encroacher (c) eaves bearer (d) listener

17. A person who has lost the protection of the law **[SSC CGL 2016]**
(a) outlaw (b) immigrant (c) outcast (d) orphan

18. Falsification of documents etc **[SSC CGL 2016]**
(a) xeroxing (b) forgery (c) laminating (d) copying

19. To make atonement for one's sins **[SSC CGL 2016]**
(a) expiate (b) renounce (c) remonstrate (d) recent

20. A rough, violent, troublesome person **[SSC CGL 2016]**
(a) tartar (b) talker (c) vagabond (d) swindler

21. A brave, nobleminded, chivalrous man **[SSC CGL 2016]**
(a) handsome (b) robust (c) gallant (d) reckless

22. Obsession with books **[SSC CGL 2016]**
(a) bibliomania (b) megalomania (c) xenophobia (d) egomania

23. Drug which causes people to sleep easily **[SSC CGL 2016]**
(a) poppy (b) soporific
(c) beguile (d) pedant

24. The branch of philosophy concerned with the study of the principles of beauty, especially in art **[SSC CGL 2016]**
(a) artistic (b) aesthetics (c) ethics (d) metaphysics

25. Highly skilled **[SSC CGL 2016]**
(a) consummate (b) inveterate (c) notorious (d) maladroit

26. Identification with the feelings of another **[SSC CGL 2016]**
(a) sympathy (b) empathy (c) apathy (d) compassion

27. Write or carve words on stone or paper **[SSC CGL 2016]**
(a) sketch (b) imprint (c) affix (d) inscribe

28. Unable to pay one's debt **[SSC CGL 2016]**
(a) insolvent (b) impute (c) indebt (d) obligate

29. Trouble and annoy continually **[SSC CGL 2016]**
(a) complaint (b) harass (c) punish (d) oppress

30. Usage of an incorrect word in place of the one which is similar in pronunciation **[SSC CGL 2016]**
(a) spoonerism (b) malapropism (c) blooper (d) corpsing

31. A person who thinks he is ill all the time **[SSC CGL 2016]**
(a) hypochondriac (b) neophyte
(c) maniac (d) misanthrope

32. A person of great learning in several languages **[SSC PO 2016, SSC CABFs 2015]**
(a) polycarp (b) polyglot (c) polychrome (d) polymath

33. A man who collects old and new coins **[SSC CGL 2016]**
(a) geologist (b) numismatist (c) archaeologist (d) zoologist

34. Regular users of places/restaurant etc **[SSC CGL 2016]**
(a) client (b) clientele (c) often (d) usage

35. One who copies from other writers **[SSC CGL 2016]**
(a) pluralist (b) imitator (c) plagiarist (d) copycat

36. A job carrying no salary **[SSC CGL Tier-I 2016]**
(a) honorary (b) memento (c) honorarium (d) memorandum

37. Act of stealing something in small quantities **[SSC CGL Tier-I 2016]**
(a) pillage (b) plagiarise
(c) proliferate (d) pilferage

38. Pertaining to the west **[SSC CGL Tier-I 2016]**
(a) celestial (b) occidental (c) oriental (d) terrestrial

39. Property inherited from one's father or ancestors **[SSC CGL Tier-I 2016]**
(a) patrimony (b) mercenary
(c) hereditary (d) aristocracy

Previous Years' Questions

40. A person who is womanish in his habits **[SSC CGL Tier-I 2016]**
(a) feminist (b) philogynist (c) effeminate (d) feminine

41. One who is converted from one religion to another **[SSC CGL Tier-I 2016]**
(a) pilgrim (b) polytheist (c) proselyte (d) presbyte

42. A brief or short stay at a place **[SSC CGL Tier-I 2016]**
(a) solitude (b) soiree (c) sojourn (d) solstice

43. One who is indifferent to pain or pleasure **[SSC CGL Tier-I 2016]**
(a) eccentric (b) philosopher (c) fatalist (d) stoic

44. An abattoir is **[SSC CHSL 2016]**
(a) a place where animals are slaughtered
(b) a place where abbots stay
(c) a title or respect given to a priest or abbot
(d) a place where animals are worshipped

45. A man with abnormal habits **[SSC CHSL 2016]**
(a) eccentric (b) frantic (c) idiotic (d) sulky

46. The belief that God is in every thing, including nature **[SSC CAPFs, SI, CISF ASI 2016]**
(a) pantheism (b) mysticism
(c) naturalism (d) polytheism

47. Gradually advanced **[SSC CAPFs SI, CISF ASI 2016]**
(a) evolved (b) evoluted
(c) evaded (d) advantaged

48. The study of growing garden plants **[SSC CAPFs (CPO) SI, CISF ASI 2016]**
(a) nursery (b) orchard
(c) nomenclature (d) horticulture

49. A person who lays too much stress on bookish learning **[SSC CGL Tier-I 2016]**
(a) pervert (b) pedant (c) philosopher (d) scholar

50. Deviation from the right course **[SSC CGL Tier-I 2016]**
(a) imagination (b) amalgamation
(c) illumination (d) aberration

ANSWERS

1 (d)	**2** (d)	**3** (c)	**4** (d)	**5** (c)	**6** (c)	**7** (b)	**8** (b)	**9** (d)	**10** (b)
11 (c)	**12** (c)	**13** (b)	**14** (c)	**15** (b)	**16** (a)	**17** (a)	**18** (b)	**19** (a)	**20** (a)
21 (c)	**22** (a)	**23** (b)	**24** (b)	**25** (a)	**26** (b)	**27** (d)	**28** (a)	**29** (b)	**30** (b)
31 (a)	**32** (b)	**33** (b)	**34** (a)	**35** (c)	**36** (a)	**37** (d)	**38** (b)	**39** (c)	**40** (c)
41 (c)	**42** (c)	**43** (d)	**44** (a)	**45** (a)	**46** (a)	**47** (a)	**48** (d)	**49** (b)	**50** (d)

One Word Substitutions

SET 3

1. A person's peculiar habit **[SSC CGL Tier-I 2016]**
(a) trait (b) idiosyncrasy (c) idiolect (d) talent

2. Speech delivered without preparation **[SSC CGL Tier-I 2016]**
(a) rhetoric (b) oration
(c) extempore (d) maiden speech

3. One who will do any job for anyone for money **[SSC CGL Tier-I 2016]**
(a) mercenary (b) recruit (c) hoodlum (d) merchant

4. Scientific study of earthquakes **[SSC CAPFs ASI 2016]**
(a) seismology (b) astrology (c) geography (d) anthropology

5. Misappropriation of money **[SSC CGL 2016]**
(a) embezzlement (b) robbery (c) theft (d) fraud

6. One who is not easily pleased by anything **[SSC CGL 2016]**
(a) gullible (b) fastidious (c) innocent (d) amenable

7. One who studies the working of the human mind
[SSC CGL Tier-I (CBE) 2016]
(a) anthropologist (b) psychologist
(c) neurologist (d) ethnologist

8. A person of South African Dutch descent **[SSC CGL Tier-I (CBE) 2016]**
(a) boar (b) boer (c) boor (d) bore

9. One who sets type for books, newspapers, etc
(a) typist (b) editor (c) composer (d) compositor

10. Lack of skill **[SSC CGL Tier-I 2016]**
(a) inertness (b) insistence (c) ineptness (d) insolence

11. Stick with a thick end used in a mortar for pounding **[SSC CGL Tier-I 2016]**
(a) thistle (b) stifle (c) sceptre (d) pestle

12. An act when people vote in order to make a decision about a particular subject or policy rather than voting for a person **[SSC CGL Tier-I 2016]**
(a) election (b) exit-poll (c) by-election (d) referendum

13. One who collects postage stamps **[SSC CAPFs SI 2016]**
(a) philanthropist (b) numismatist (c) philatelist (d) curator

14. Nations that do not trust each other/look upon each other
[SSC CAPFs 2016]
(a) calmly (b) hopefully (c) askance (d) retrospectively

15. One of the time tested ways of remembering a series of items
[SSC CAPFs 2016]
(a) recollection (b) schematising (c) mnemonic (d) ingenuity

Previous Years' Questions

16. Bitter and violent attack in words? **[SSC CAPFs 2016]**
(a) diaspora (b) diacriticism
(c) diadem (d) diatribe

17. Head of monks in an abbey **[SSC CGL Tier-II 2016]**
(a) padre (b) dean (c) abbot (d) deacon

18. The word is no longer in use **[SSC CGL Tier-II 2016]**
(a) obsolete (b) old fashion (c) antique (d) vanished

19. A person unselfishly concerned for or devoted to the welfare of others **[SSC CGL Tier-II 2016]**
(a) egoist (b) unselfish (c) altruist (d) welfarist

20. Inscription on a gravestone **[SSC CGL Tier-II 2016]**
(a) obituary (b) memorial (c) epitaph (d) epigraph

21. Violation of that which is holy and sacred **[SSC CGL Tier-II 2016]**
(a) malevolent (b) sacrilege (c) bizarre (d) iniquitous

22. One who believes in many Gods **[SSC CGL Tier-II 2016]**
(a) polyglot (b) polygamy
(c) polygon (d) polytheist

23. One who lends money on high rate of interest **[SSC CGL Tier-II 2016]**
(a) usurper (b) usherer (c) usurer (d) undertaker

24. A post with little work but high salary **[SSC CGL Tier-II 2016]**
(a) freelancer (b) sine qua non (c) sinecure (d) quangos

25. A person, especially a young, one with exceptional abilities **[SSC CGL Tier-II 2016]**
(a) intellectual (b) prodigy (c) genius (d) mastermind

26. Incapable of feeling tired or exhausted **[SSC CGL Tier-II 2016]**
(a) invincible (b) inflatable (c) indefatigable (d) inextricable

27. A new word coined by an author **[SSC CGL Tier-II 2016]**
(a) novelty (b) innovation (c) neologism (d) inception

28. A place where astronomical observations are made **[SSC CGL Tier-I 2016]**
(a) astrophery (b) laboratory (c) observatory (d) astrolibrary

29. Killing one's sister **[SSC CGL 2016]**
(a) regicide (b) fratricide (c) matricide (d) sororicide

30. Experts who scientifically study insects **[SSC CGL 2016]**
(a) gerontologists (b) pathologists
(c) entomologists (d) ornithologist

31. A person's peculiar habit **[SSC CGL 2016]**
(a) peculiarity (b) trait
(c) distinction (d) idiosyncrasy

32. A narrow stretch of land connecting two large bodies of land **[SSC CGL 2016]**
(a) lagoon (b) isthumas (c) cape (d) strait

33. A government or rule by a small group of people **[SSC CGL 2016]**
(a) monarchy (b) oligarchy (c) autocracy (d) autonomy

34. The scientific study of elections **[SSC CGL 2016]**
(a) pathology (b) palaeontology (c) psephology (d) philology

35. A doctor who specialises in the diseases of the eyes **[SSC CGL 2016]**
(a) opthalmologist (b) optimist
(c) optician (d) orthodontist

36. Person who eats too much **[SSC CGL 2016]**
(a) cannibal (b) glutton (c) obese (d) carnivorous

37. Proposition made as a basis for reasoning without the assumption of its truth **[SSC CGL Tier-I 2016]**
(a) hypertext (b) hypocrisy (c) hyperbole (d) hypothesis

38. A child born after the death of father **[SSC CGL Tier-I 2016]**
(a) post dated (b) premature (c) paternal (d) posthumous

39. A person who completely abstains from alcohol **[SSC CGL Tier-I 2016]**
(a) teetotaller (b) drunkard (c) alcoholic (d) imposter

40. One who is able to use both hands **[SSC CGL Tier-I 2016]**
(a) sinister (b) ambidextrous (c) ambivalent (d) amateur

41. The ceremony of crowning a sovereign **[SSC CGL Tier-I 2016]**
(a) felicitation (b) promotion (c) coronation (d) installation

42. One who tends to patronise, rebuff or ignore people regarded as social inferiors and imitate, admire people regarded as social superiors **[SSC CGL Tier-I 2016]**
(a) snob (b) fob (c) dandy (d) freak

43. A room where dead bodies are kept until burial
(a) grave (b) cemetery (c) mortuary (d) pyre

44. Animals without a backbone **[SSC CGL Tier-I 2016]**
(a) marsupials (b) mammals (c) vertebrate (d) invertebrates

45. The act of killing a king **[SSC CGL Tier-I CBE 2016]**
(a) regicide (b) regalcide (c) genocide (d) homicide

46. Emission of light or heat from a central point **[SSC CGL Tier-I CBE 2016]**
(a) rays (b) refraction (c) reflection (d) radiation

47. Any morbid dread of water **[SSC CGL 2016]**
(a) hydrofoil (b) hydrophobia
(c) hydraulic (d) hyacinth

48. A drug which makes one see things that are not really there **[SSC CGL Tier-I 2016]**
(a) aphrodisiac (b) steroid (c) carcinogen (d) hallucinogen

49. Providing relief **[SSC CGL Tier-I 2016]**
(a) reissue (b) reprieve (c) rejoinder (d) refuge

50. The philosophy of putting another's welfare above one's own **[SSC CGL Tier-I 2016]**
(a) agnosticism (b) polytheism (c) altruism (d) iconoclasm

ANSWERS

1 *(b)*	**2** *(c)*	**3** *(a)*	**4** *(a)*	**5** *(a)*	**6** *(b)*	**7** *(b)*	**8** *(b)*	**9** *(d)*	**10** *(c)*
11 *(d)*	**12** *(d)*	**13** *(b)*	**14** *(c)*	**15** *(c)*	**16** *(d)*	**17** *(c)*	**18** *(a)*	**19** *(c)*	**20** *(c)*
21 *(b)*	**22** *(d)*	**23** *(c)*	**24** *(c)*	**25** *(b)*	**26** *(c)*	**27** *(c)*	**28** *(c)*	**29** *(d)*	**30** *(c)*
31 *(d)*	**32** *(b)*	**33** *(b)*	**34** *(c)*	**35** *(a)*	**36** *(b)*	**37** *(d)*	**38** *(d)*	**39** *(a)*	**40** *(b)*
41 *(c)*	**42** *(a)*	**43** *(c)*	**44** *(d)*	**45** *(a)*	**46** *(d)*	**47** *(b)*	**48** *(d)*	**49** *(b)*	**50** *(c)*

SET 4

1. That which makes one highly knowledgeable **[SSC CGL Tier-I 2016]**
(a) erudition (b) irreverence (c) irritability (d) impulsiveness

2. Violation of the sanctity of a sacred place **[SSC CGL Tier-I 2016]**
(a) sin (b) sacrilege (c) sedition (d) blasphemy

3. Not suitable for eating **[SSC CGL Tier-I 2015]**
(a) spicy (b) tasteless (c) uneatable (d) inedible

4. When something moves in a straight line **[SSC CGL Tier-II 2016]**
(a) quadrilineal (b) octalineal (c) rectilineal (d) trapilineal

5. Tending to associate with others of one's kind **[SSC CGL Tier-II 2016]**
(a) grassivorous (b) gregarian (c) gregarious (d) graminivorous

6. General pardon for offences against the state **[SSC CGL Tier-II 2016]**
(a) sanctify (b) amnesty (c) gratuity (d) red-tapism

7. A person motivated by irrational enthusiasm **[SSC CGL Tier-II 2016]**
(a) moderate (b) conservative (c) fanatic (d) fan

8. Wide, uninterrupted view **[SSC CGL Tier-II 2016]**
(a) window view (b) panorama (c) macroscopic (d) eagle view

9. An instrument for measuring pressure of gases **[SSC CGL Tier-II 2016]**
(a) barometer (b) anemometer (c) micrometer (d) manometer

10. That cannot be expressed in words **[SSC CGL Tier-II 2016]**
(a) indelible (b) ineffable (c) ingrate (d) inexorable

11. A mixture of dried, naturally fragrant plant material used to provide a gentle natural scent inside buildings, especially in residential settings **[SSC CGL Tier-II 2016]**
(a) potpourri (b) perfume (c) scent (d) aroma

12. Placing different things in order to create an interesting effect **[SSC CGL Tier-II 2016]**
(a) sit for a portrait (b) render precisely
(c) juxtapose (d) framing

13. Study of cultures **[SSC CGL Tier-II 2016]**
(a) eremology (b) etymology (c) ethology (d) ethnology

14. A lengthy and aggressive speech addressed to a large assembly **[SSC CGL Tier-II 2016]**
(a) hullabaloo (b) cacophony (c) pandemonium (d) harangue

15. Bare minimum needed for survival **[SSC CGL 2016]**
(a) sustenance (b) subsistence (c) substainable (d) supplement

16. Act of mercy killing **[SSC CGL 2016]**
(a) suicide (b) euthanasia (c) immolation (d) asphyxiation

17. Action that is likely to make people angry **[SSC CGL 2016]**
(a) inflationary (b) inflammable (c) commensurable (d) inflammatory

18. A person who wastes his money on luxury **[SSC CGL Tier-II 2015]**
(a) luxuriant (b) stingy (c) extravagant (d) luxurious

19. Edible means that which **[SSC CGL Tier-II 2015]**
(a) can be edited (b) can not be deleted
(c) edifying (d) is worth eating

20. A written declaration of government or a political party **[SSC CGL Tier-II 2015]**
(a) manifesto (b) affidavit
(c) dossier (d) document

21. One who is rather fastidious **[SSC CGL Tier-II 2015]**
(a) tempestuous (b) punctual (c) meticulous (d) carefree

22. Branch of medicine concerned with children and their illness **[SSC CGL Tier-II 2015]**
(a) cardiology (b) osteopathy
(c) pediatrics (d) morphology

23. Government by the wealthy **[SSC CGL Tier-II 2015]**
(a) theocracy (b) plutocracy
(c) bureaucracy (d) aristocracy

24. People at a religious gathering **[SSC CGL Tier-II 2015]**
(a) rabble (b) mob (c) congregation (d) crowd

Previous Years' Questions

25. A person who collects and/or studies stamps **[SSC CGL Tier-II 2015]**
(a) pioneer (b) philatelist (c) pianist (d) philanthropist

26. Information about the bird species was **inaccessible**. One has to access rare websites to access it **[SSC CGL Tier-II 2015]**
The meaning of the **bold** word is
(a) that which cannot be read
(b) that which cannot be reached
(c) that which cannot be remembered
(d) that which cannot be stretched

27. Guilty of the crime **[SSC CGL Tier-II 2015, SSC CHSL 2014]**
(a) daring (b) suspicious (c) culpable (d) ruthless

28. A fourteen-line poem **[SSC CGL Tier-II 2015]**
(a) sonnet (b) lyric (c) ballad (d) ode

29. The plants and vegetation of a region **[SSC CGL Tier-II 2015]**
(a) flora (b) landscape (c) environment (d) fauna

30. A vivacious and lively experience is said to be **[SSC CGL Tier-II 2015]**
(a) scintillating (b) soothing (c) scenic (d) synthetic

31. To try to settle a dispute between two other parties **[SSC CGL Tier-II 2015]**
(a) medicate (b) mediate (c) meddle (d) meditate

32. To secure a boat by attaching it to an anchor **[SSC CGL Tier-II 2015]**
(a) moor (b) moot (c) morose (d) moose

33. To free a person by a verdict of 'not guilty'. **[SSC CGL Tier-II 2015]**
(a) acquaint (b) acquit (c) acquiesce (d) acquire

34. One who hates mankind **[SSC CGL Tier-II 2015]**
(a) philanthropist (b) misogynist (c) humanitarian (d) misanthrope

35. Imposed a restriction on **[SSC CGL Tier-II 2015]**
(a) constipated (b) conserved (c) constrained (d) construed

36. Unwelcome aspect of a situation **[SSC CGL Tier-II 2015]**
(a) flippant (b) flip side (c) flip-flop (d) flint lock

37. Feeling annoyed at the sight of unfair treatment **[SSC CGL Tier-II 2015]**
(a) indifferent (b) indisposed (c) indignant (d) indigent

38. Medical study of skin and its diseases **[SSC CGL Tier-I 2015]**
(a) orthopaedics (b) dermatology
(c) endocrinology (d) gynaecology

39. A process involving too much official formality **[SSC CGL Tier-I 2015]**
(a) nepotism (b) diplomacy
(c) bureaucracy (d) red-tapism

40. A person who enters without any invitation **[SSC CGL Tier-I 2015]**
(a) vandal (b) burglar
(c) intruder (d) thief

41. A recurrent compulsive urge to steal **[SSC CGL Tier-I 2015]**
(a) kleptomania (b) pneumonia
(c) insomnia (d) nymphomania

42. Act of injuring another's reputation by any slanderous communication **[SSC CGL Tier-I 2015]**
(a) defamation (b) orchestration
(c) aberration (d) misrepresentation

43. A study of ancient things **[SSC CGL Tier-I 2015]**
(a) physiology (b) archaeology
(c) ethnology (d) zoology

44. A person who deserves all praise **[SSC CGL Tier-I 2015]**
(a) detestable (b) lovable (c) despicable (d) laudable

45. One who is skilful **[SSC CGL Tier-I 2015]**
(a) disciplined (b) diligent (c) different (d) dexterous

46. One who runs away from justice or the law **[SSC CGL Tier-I 2015]**
(a) smuggler (b) criminal (c) fugitive (d) thief

47. Of one's own free will **[SSC CGL Tier-I 2015]**
(a) mandatory (b) obligatory (c) voluntary (d) compulsory

48. One who is too careless to plan for the future **[SSC CGL Tier-I 2015]**
(a) imprudent (b) impractical (c) impotent (d) improvident

49. One who has long experience **[SSC CGL Tier-I 2015]**
(a) novice (b) expert (c) veteran (d) practitioner

50. Walking in sleep **[SSC CARFs SI, & Delhi Police SI 2015]**
(a) somnambulism (b) insomnia
(c) somnolence (d) sleepyhead

ANSWERS

1 *(a)*	**2** *(b)*	**3** *(d)*	**4** *(c)*	**5** *(c)*	**6** *(b)*	**7** *(c)*	**8** *(c)*	**9** *(d)*	**10** *(b)*
11 *(a)*	**12** *(c)*	**13** *(d)*	**14** *(d)*	**15** *(b)*	**16** *(b)*	**17** *(d)*	**18** *(c)*	**19** *(d)*	**20** *(a)*
21 *(c)*	**22** *(c)*	**23** *(b)*	**24** *(c)*	**25** *(b)*	**26** *(b)*	**27** *(c)*	**28** *(a)*	**29** *(a)*	**30** *(a)*
31 *(b)*	**32** *(a)*	**33** *(b)*	**34** *(b)*	**35** *(c)*	**36** *(b)*	**37** *(c)*	**38** *(b)*	**39** *(d)*	**40** *(c)*
41 *(a)*	**42** *(a)*	**43** *(b)*	**44** *(d)*	**45** *(d)*	**46** *(c)*	**47** *(c)*	**48** *(a)*	**49** *(c)*	**50** *(a)*

Previous Years' Questions

SET 5

1. Artistic, musical or dramatic interpretation **[SSC CARFs SI, CISF ASI 2015]**
(a) rendition (b) report (c) imitation (d) reparation

2. That which cannot be avoided **[SSC CARFs SI, CISF ASI 2015]**
(a) infallible (b) inestimable (c) indifferent (d) inevitable

3. A person who leaves his own country in order to go and live in another **[SSC CARFs SI & Delhi Police SI 2015]**
(a) emigrant (b) refugee (c) immigrant (d) expatriate

4. A planned route or journey **[SSC CARFs SI, CISF ASI 2015]**
(a) iterate (b) itinerary (c) itinerant (d) isolate

5. A man who helps a stranger or a person in difficulties **[SSC CARFs SI & Delhi Police SI 2015]**
(a) samaritan (b) mercenary (c) stoic (d) altruist

6. Speech of great importance and gravity **[SSC CARFs SI, CISF ASI 2015]**
(a) maiden (b) momentous
(c) monumental (d) momentary

7. Continuing for a long period of time without interruption **[SSC CARFs SI & Delhi Police SI 2015]**
(a) continuum (b) recurring (c) perpetual (d) frequenting

8. Specially skilled in story-telling **[SSC CARFs SI 2015]**
(a) compositor (b) raconteur (c) vocalist (d) narrator

9. A story in which animals or objects speak and give wholesome moral lesson **[SSC CARFs SI, CISF ASI & Delhi Police SI 2015]**
(a) legend (b) fable (c) parable (d) allegory

10. A cinema show held in the afternoon **[SSC CHSL (10+2) LDC, DEO & PA/SA 2015]**
(a) entertainment (b) play (c) premiere (d) matinee

11. A handsome man **[SSC CHSL (10+2) LDC, DEO & PA/SA 2015]**
(a) adonis (b) tycoon (c) debonair (d) cavalier

12. Intentional damage to arrest production **[SSC CHSL (10+2) LDC, DEO & PA/SA 2015]**
(a) nemesis (b) sangfroid
(c) sabotage (d) modus operandi

13. Introductory part or lines to a discourse or play **[SSC CHSL (10+2) LDC, DEO & PA/SA 2015]**
(a) prologue (b) blurb (c) monologue (d) epilogue

14. One who does not believe in the existence of God **[SSC CGL Tier-I 2015]**
(a) atheist (b) theist (c) mystic (d) cynic

15. To free someone from all blames **[SSC CGL Tier-I 2015]**
(a) consolidate (b) fling (c) forbid (d) exonerate

16. That which cannot be effaced **[SSC CGL Tier-I 2015]**
(a) illegible (b) indelible (c) invincible (d) affable

17. A person who deliberately sets fire to a building **[SSC CGL Tier-I 2015]**
(a) arsonist (b) extortionist (c) hijacker (d) assassin

18. One who makes an official examination of accounts **[SSC CGL Tier-I 2015]**
(a) auditor (b) registrar
(c) creditor (d) chartered accountant

19. Conferred as an honour **[SSC CGL Tier-I 2015]**
(a) honorary (b) honorable (c) honorarium (d) honorific

20. The burial of a corpse **[SSC CGL Tier-I 2015]**
(a) internment (b) interment (c) interrogate (d) interpose

21. To die without making a will **[SSC CGL Tier-I 2015]**
(a) inure (b) inane (c) intestate (d) indigent

22. Materials that change naturally by the action of bacteria **[SSC CGL Tier-I 2015]**
(a) inflammable (b) perishable (c) biological (d) biodegradable

23. A person who agrees to work for somebody in order to learn a skill **[SSC CGL Tier-I 2015]**
(a) lackey (b) pupil (c) apprentice (d) assistant

24. Opinion contrary to accepted doctrines **[SSC CGL Tier-I 2015]**
(a) controversy (b) advocacy (c) heresy (d) convention

25. Make pale by excluding light **[SSC CGL Tier-I 2015]**
(a) foliate (b) percolate (c) procreate (d) etiolate

26. Someone who is designated to hear both sides of a dispute and make a judgement **[SSC CGL Tier-I 2015]**
(a) counsellor (b) arbitrator (c) magistrate (d) manager

27. A person who looks at the bright side of things **[SSC CAPFs SI, CISF ASI 2015]**
(a) cynic (b) pessimist (c) optimist (d) sycophant

28. A record of historical events **[SSC CAPFs SI, CISF ASI 2015]**
(a) documentary (b) anecdotes (c) archives (d) annals

29. The area of medicine that treats illnesses of bones **[SSC CAPFs SI, CISF ASI 2015]**
(a) ornithology (b) paediatrics (c) orthodontics (d) orthopaedics

30. A reserve for animals, birds, etc in their natural habitat **[SSC CAPFs SI, CISF ASI & Delhi Police SI 2015]**
(a) sanctuary (b) century (c) forest (d) woods

Previous Years' Questions

31. Something that is difficult to understand **[SSC CGL Tier-I Re-Exam 2015]**
(a) incomplete (b) inconclusive
(c) inconceivable (d) incomprehensible

32. That which is arranged by conferring of discussing **[SSC CGL Tier-I Re-Exam 2015]**
(a) meeting (b) seminar (c) debate (d) negotiation

33. A mournful poem or a song **[SSC CGL Tier-I Re-Exam 2015]**
(a) comedy (b) tragedy (c) elegy (d) ode

34. An image without objective reality **[SSC CGL Tier-I Re-Exam 2015]**
(a) shadow (b) utopia (c) sensation (d) hallucination

35. The branch of medical science which deals with the problems of the old **[SSC CGL Tier-I Re-Exam 2015]**
(a) oncology (b) obstetrics (c) paediatrics (d) geriatrics

36. A child secretly changed for another in infancy **[SSC CGL Tier-I Re-Exam 2015]**
(a) nipper (b) changeling (c) tiddler (d) tyke

37. One who suffers for one's faith **[SSC CGL Tier-I Re-Exam 2015]**
(a) prophet (b) mystic (c) seer (d) martyr

38. Put side by side **[SSC Constable (GD) 2015]**
(a) juxtapose (b) impose (c) propose (d) depose

39. One who can not be corrected **[SSC Constable (GD) 2015]**
(a) ineligible (b) indolent (c) indefatigable (d) incorrigible

40. Chief or Commander of army **[SSC Constable (GD) 2015]**
(a) lieutenant (b) major (c) general (d) colonel

41. A container for the ashes of a dead person **[SSC Constable (GD) 2015]**
(a) vessel (b) vase (c) jug (d) urn

42. Someone not fit to be chosen **[SSC CHSL (10+2) LDC, DEO & PA/SA 2015]**
(a) non-eligible (b) ineligible
(c) uneligible (d) imeligible

43. One who compiles a dictionary **[SSC CHSL (10+2) LDC, DEO & PA/SA 2015]**
(a) lexicon (b) lexical (c) lexicography (d) lexicographer

44. Art of working with metals **[SSC CHSL LDC 2016)**
(a) meteorite (b) metaphysics (c) metallurgy (d) metalloid

45. Rules governing socially acceptable behaviour **[SSC CHSL (10+2) LDC, DEO & PA/SA 2015]**
(a) politeness (b) formality (c) behaviour (d) etiquette

46. A person who is easily deceived or tricked **[SSC CHSL (10+2) LDC, DEO & PA/SA 2015]**
(a) tangible (b) trouble (c) trickster (d) gullible

47. Lasting for a very short time **[SSC CHSL (10+2) LDC, DEO& PA/SA 2015]**
(a) metronimic (b) friable (c) eternal (d) ephemeral

48. A person who worships only one God **[SSC CHSL (10+2) LDC, DEO & PA/SA 2015]**
(a) polytheist (b) monotheist (c) philogymist (d) theist

49. A person who helps another to commit a crime **[SSC CHSL (10+2) LDC, DEO & PA/SA 2015]**
(a) colleague (b) accomplice (c) assistant (d) supporter

50. A legal agreement that allows someone to use a building or land for a period of time, usually in return for rent **[SSC CHSL (10+2) LDC, DEO & PA/SA 2015]**
(a) assurance (b) deal (c) lease (d) bond

ANSWERS

1 *(a)*	**2** *(d)*	**3** *(a)*	**4** *(b)*	**5** *(a)*	**6** *(b)*	**7** *(c)*	**8** *(b)*	**9** *(b)*	**10** *(d)*
11 *(a)*	**12** *(c)*	**13** *(a)*	**14** *(a)*	**15** *(d)*	**16** *(b)*	**17** *(a)*	**18** *(a)*	**19** *(a)*	**20** *(b)*
21 *(c)*	**22** *(d)*	**23** *(d)*	**24** *(c)*	**25** *(d)*	**26** *(b)*	**27** *(c)*	**28** *(c)*	**29** *(d)*	**30** *(a)*
31 *(d)*	**32** *(d)*	**33** *(c)*	**34** *(d)*	**35** *(d)*	**36** *(b)*	**37** *(d)*	**38** *(a)*	**39** *(d)*	**40** *(c)*
41 *(d)*	**42** *(b)*	**43** *(d)*	**44** *(c)*	**45** *(d)*	**46** *(d)*	**47** *(d)*	**48** *(b)*	**49** *(b)*	**50** *(c)*

SET 6

1. The act of killing one's own brother or sister
(a) homicide (b) suicide (c) patricide (d) fratricide

2. Submission to all that happens as inevitable **[SSC CHSL (10+2) LDC, DEO & PA/SA 2015]**
(a) pessimism (b) pragmatism (c) fatalism (d) superstiticism

3. Feint **[SSC CAPFs 2015]**
(a) pretended effect (b) pretended attack
(c) pretended effort (d) pretended support

4. A person who is long experienced or practised in an activity/capacity **[SSC CAPFs 2015]**
(a) veteran (b) versatile (c) vulnerable (d) venerable

5. An excessive fear of confined spaces **[SSC CAPFs 2015]**
(a) hydrophobia (b) bathophobia
(c) cynophobia (d) claustrophobia

6. A person in charge of a museum **[SSC CHSL LDC 2015]**
(a) architect (b) mayor (c) philatelist (d) curator

7. The first public showing of a film **[SSC CHSL LDC 2015]**
(a) opener (b) premiere (c) debut (d) preview

Previous Years' Questions

8. Too willing to obey other people **[SCC CGL Tier-II 2015]**
(a) sublimate (b) subjugate (c) subaltern (d) subservient

9. A person extremely desirous of money **[SCC CGL Tier-II 2015]**
(a) miser (b) avaricious (c) fervent (d) extravagant

10. An error or misprint in printing or writing **[SCC CGL Tier-II 2015]**
(a) agenda (b) axiom (c) erratum (d) jargon

11. A person who is very selective, disgusted easily, and is hard to please. **[SCC CGL Tier-II 2015]**
(a) fastidious (b) ambiguous (c) selector (d) misanthrope

12. The period between two reigns **[SCC CGL Tier-II 2015]**
(a) anachronism (b) interregnum (c) intermission (d) era

13. A statement in which you say the same thing twice in different words **[SCC CGL Tier-II 2015]**
(a) temerity (b) tarragon (c) tautology (d) repetition

14. One who is known widely but usually unfavourably **[SCC CGL Tier-II 2015]**
(a) famous (b) illustrious (c) notorious (d) tarnished

15. A person who has had one or more limbs removed **[SCC CGL Tier-II 2015]**
(a) amputee (b) handicap (c) limber (d) fatalist

16. To destroy completely **[SCC CGL Tier-II 2015]**
(a) bluster (b) chide (c) dawdle (d) annihilate

17. House or shelter of a gypsie **[SSC CAPFs 2014]**
(a) wigwam (b) chalet (c) caravan (d) igloo

18. A woman whose husband is dead **[SSC CAPFs SI, 2014]**
(a) divorcee (b) fiancee (c) widower (d) widow

19. One who eats no animal flesh **[SSC CAPFs SI 2014]**
(a) cannibal (b) pilgrim (c) vegetarian (d) pedestrian

20. Water which can be drunk **[SSC CAPFs SI & Delhi Police SI 2014]**
(a) edible (b) potable (c) palatable (d) culpable

21. One who is neither intelligent nor dull **[SSC CAPFs SI & Delhi Police SI 2014]**
(a) ordinary (b) average (c) fair (d) mediocre

22. A small village or a group of houses **[SSC CAPFs SI & Delhi Police SI 2014]**
(a) community (b) settlement (c) hamlet (d) colony

23. A decorative ring of flowers and leaves **[SSC Multitasking 2014]**
(a) wreathe (b) wreath (c) wreeth (d) wrath

24. A heavy continuous fall of rain **[SSC Multitasking 2014]**
(a) drizzle (b) blizzard
(c) downpour (d) avalanche

25. Completing a period of hundred years **[SSC Multitasking Staff 2014]**
(a) centennial (b) centurion (c) century (d) centenarian

26. A game in which no one wins **[SSC Multitasking Stoff 2014]**
(a) draw (b) obsolete
(c) legal (d) illegal

27. Shaking movement on the ground **[SSC Multitasking Staff 2014]**
(a) tremor (b) shiver (c) vibrate (d) oscillate

28. An extract from a book of writing **[SSC CGL Tier-I 2014]**
(a) excerpt (b) review (c) footnote (d) preface

29. A long poem based or a noble theme **[SSC CGL Tier-I 2014]**
(a) summary (b) story (c) narration (d) epic

30. Widespread scarcity of food **[SSC CHSL (10+2) DEO & LDC 2014]**
(a) hunger (b) drought (c) poverty (d) famine

31. Inflammation of gums **[SSC CHSL (10+2) DEO & LDC 2014]**
(a) gangerene (b) gingivitis (c) conjunctivitis (d) orchitis

32. A book written by an unknown author **[SSC CHSL (10+2) DEO & LDC 2014]**
(a) anonymous (b) acrimonious (c) audacious (d) assiduous

33. An event that causes great harm to dams
[SSC CHSL (10+2) DEO & LDC 2014]
(a) problem (b) disaster
(c) pain (d) relief

34. Beyond correction **[SSC CHSL (10+2) DEO & LDC 2014]**
(a) inveterate (b) glib (c) incorrigible (d) incongruous

35. An allowance made to a wife by her husband, when they are legally separated **[SSC CHSL (10+2) DEO & LDC 2014]**
(a) alimony (b) parsimony (c) matrimony (d) honorarium

36. Wild imagination **[SSC CHSL (10+2) DEO & LDC 2014]**
(a) whim (b) fantasy (c) fancy (d) memory

37. Sentimental longing for a period in the past
[SSC CHSL (10+2) DEO & LDC 2014]
(a) recollection (b) nostalgia (c) reminiscence (d) wistfulness

38. The headmaster **brought back to mind** the outstanding achievements of the school **[SSC CHSL (10+2) DEO & LDC 2014]**
(a) remembered (b) reminded (c) reminisced (d) recalled

39. Lack of feeling **[SSC CHSL (10+2) DEO & LDC 2014]**
(a) empathy (b) apathy (c) sympathy (d) pity

40. Accidental good fortune **[SSC CHSL (10+2) DEO & LDC 2014]**
(a) serendipity (b) good luck (c) chance (d) fluke

Previous Years' Questions

41. Short speech or poem given at the end of a play or a book **[SSC CHSL (10+2) DEO & LDC 2014]**

(a) epilogue (b) epigram (c) epitaph (d) epicure

42. The secretary's proposal was adopted **with the full agreement of all the members.** **[SSC CHSL (10+2) DEO & LDC 2014]**

(a) ambitiously (b) unanimously (c) equivocally (d) vehemently

43. That which makes it difficult to recognise the presence or real nature of something **[SSC CHSL (10+2) DEO & LDC 2014]**

(a) camouflage (b) transparent (c) infallible (d) image

44. Code of diplomatic etiquette and precedence **[SSC CHSL (10+2) DEO & LDC 2014]**

(a) formality (b) statesmanship (c) protocol (d) hierarchy

45. A person who can make himself/ herself feel at home in any country **[SSC CHSL (10+2) DEO & LDC 2014]**

(a) cosmocrat (b) cosmesis (c) cosmetician (d) cosmopolitan

46. The Bedouin Arabs are people of no fixed abode **[SSC CHSL (10+2) DEO & LDC 2014]**

(a) barbarians (b) nomads
(c) vagabonds (d) travellers

47. Study of the interaction of people with their environment **[SSC Graduate Level Tier-II 2014]**

(a) ecology (b) psychology
(c) philosophy (d) geography

48. A list of explanations of rare, technical or obsolete words **[SSC Graduate Level Tier-II 2014]**

(a) dictionary (b) glossary (c) lexicon (d) catalogue

49. Underground place for storing wine or other provisions **[SSC Graduate Level Tier-II 2014]**

(a) garage (b) cellar (c) attic (d) hall

50. Free somebody from blame or guilt **[SSC Graduate Level Tier-II 2014]**

(a) excuse (b) reprimand (c) exonerate (d) acquit

ANSWERS

1 *(d)*	**2** *(c)*	**3** *(b)*	**4** *(a)*	**5** *(d)*	**6** *(d)*	**7** *(b)*	**8** *(d)*	**9** *(b)*	**10** *(c)*
11 *(a)*	**12** *(b)*	**13** *(c)*	**14** *(c)*	**15** *(a)*	**16** *(d)*	**17** *(c)*	**18** *(d)*	**19** *(c)*	**20** *(b)*
21 *(d)*	**22** *(c)*	**23** *(b)*	**24** *(c)*	**25** *(a)*	**26** *(a)*	**27** *(a)*	**28** *(a)*	**29** *(d)*	**30** *(d)*
31 *(b)*	**32** *(a)*	**33** *(b)*	**34** *(c)*	**35** *(a)*	**36** *(b)*	**37** *(b)*	**38** *(d)*	**39** *(b)*	**40** *(d)*
41 *(a)*	**42** *(b)*	**43** *(a)*	**44** *(b)*	**45** *(d)*	**46** *(b)*	**47** *(a)*	**48** *(c)*	**49** *(b)*	**50** *(c)*

One Word Substitutions

SET 7

1. One who plays for pleasure rather than as profession **[SSC Graduate Level Tier-II 2014]**
   (a) player (b) amateur (c) performer (d) actor

2. One who does something for the first time **[SSC Graduate Level Tier-II 2014]**
   (a) leader (b) model (c) forerunner (d) pioneer

3. A government run by officials **[SSC Graduate Level Tier-II 2014]**
   (a) democracy (b) anarchy (c) oligarchy (d) bureaucracy

4. That which can not be called back **[SSC Graduate Level Tier-II 2014]**
   (a) irresponsible (b) irrevocable (c) irredeemable (d) incalculable

5. Person leading a life a strict self-discipline **[SSC Graduate Level Tier-II 2014]**
   (a) hedonist (b) disciplinarian (c) atheist (d) ascetic

6. A person who loves everybody **[SSC Graduate Level Tier-II 2014]**
   (a) egoist (b) fatalist (c) humanist (d) altruist

7. Animals which suckle their young **[SSC CHSL (10+2) DEO & LDC 2014]**
   (a) herbivores (b) mammals (c) carnivores (d) omnivores

8. A drug or other substance that induces sleep **[SSC CHSL (10+2) DEO & LDC (Nov) 2014]**
   (a) reviver (b) stimulant (c) energic (d) sedative

9. Animals that eat flesh **[SSC CHSL (10+2) DEO & LDC 2014]**
   (a) herbivorous (b) carnivorous (c) omnivorous (d) insectivorous

10. A fictitious name especially one assumed by an author **[SSC CHSL (10+2) DEO & LDC 2014]**
    (a) nick name (b) pseudonym (c) sobriquet (d) pet name

11. Belief in many gods **[SSC CGL Tier-I 2014]**
    (a) pantheism (b) monotheism (c) polytheism (d) atheism

12. A cluster of flowers on a branch **[SSC CGL Tier-I 2014]**
    (a) bouquet (b) inflorescence (c) wreath (d) incandescence

13. A person who believes that only selfishness motivates human actions **[SSC CGL Tier-I 2014]**
    (a) agnostic (b) cynic (c) sceptic (d) misogynist

14. A person who always runs after women **[SSC CAPFs SI Delhi Police SI 2014]**
    (a) philanthropist (b) don juan casanova
    (c) philanderer (d) philatelist

15. Man who has more than one wife at a time **[SSC CAPFs SI, CISF ASI 2014]**
    (a) celibate (b) bigamist (c) misogamist (d) polygamist

Previous Years' Questions

16. One who deals in flowers **[SSC CAPFs SI, CISF ASI & Delhi Police 2014]**
(a) a drover (b) a brazier (c) a florist (d) a fruiterer

17. The art of making maps and charts **[SSC Multitasking Staff 2014]**
(a) calligraphy (b) palaeography (c) metallurgy (d) cartography

18. A figure with many angles or sides **[SSC Multitasking Staff 2014]**
(a) hexagon (b) octagon (c) polygon (d) pentagon

19. The firing of many guns at the same time to mark an occasion **[SSC CGL Tier-I 2014]**
(a) fusillade (b) salvo (c) attack (d) volley

20. A word that reads the same backwards as forwards **[SSC CGL Tier-I 2014]**
(a) acrostic (b) homophone (c) acronym (d) palindrome

21. A collection of slaves **[SSC CAPFs SI, CISF ASI 2014]**
(a) coffle (b) crew (c) cortege (d) company

22. One who is always doubting **[SSC CAPFs SI, CISF ASI 2014]**
(a) sceptic (b) deist (c) rationalist (d) positivist

23. A policy that segregates people on the basis of race **[SSC CHSL (10+2) DEO & LDC 2014]**
(a) chauvinism (b) theism (c) apartheid (d) partisan

24. Design made by putting together coloured pieces of glass or stones **[SSC CHSL (10+2) DEO & LDC 2014]**
(a) tracery (b) mosaic (c) relief (d) oleograph

25. A fear of closed/dark place **[SSC CHSL (10+2) DEO & LDC 2014]**
(a) xenophobia (b) acrophobia
(c) claustrophobia (d) pyrophobia

26. Fear of telling lies **[SSC CHSL (10+2) DEO & LDC 2014]**
(a) mythophobia (b) legendary
(c) lyophobia (d) oratory

27. A particular method of working **[SSC CHSL (10+2) DEO & LDC 2014]**
(a) methodology (b) knack
(c) working pattern (d) modus operandi

28. A highly skilled musician **[SSC CGL Tier-I 2014]**
(a) artiste (b) virtuoso (c) performer (d) diva

29. A method of boiling briefly to cook food slightly **[SSC CGL Tier-I 2014]**
(a) steam (b) bake (c) saute (d) parboil

30. The group, especially in the arts, regarded as being the most experimental **[SSC CGL Tier-I 2014]**
(a) avant-garde (b) iconoclast
(c) revolutionary (d) nerd

31. One who helps people by giving them money or other aid **[SSC CGL Tier-I 2014]**
(a) benefactor (b) beneficiary (c) tycoon (d) patriot

32. Study of caves **[SSC CGL Tier-I 2014]**
(a) speleology (b) seismology (c) topology (d) numismatics

33. Government by the few **[SSC CGL Tier-I 2014]**
(a) oligarchy (b) autocracy (c) monarchy (d) anarchy

34. Having a stale smell or taste **[SSC CGL Tier-I 2014]**
(a) rancid (b) insipid (c) savoury (d) tepid

35. A wooden object used for connecting animals that are pulling a vehicle **[SSC CGL Tier-I 2014]**
(a) rein (b) leash (c) whip (d) yoke

36. A man who knows a lot about things like food, music and art **[SSC CGL Tier-I 2014]**
(a) priest (b) optimist (c) hostage (d) connoisseur

37. A doctor who specialises in diseases of the nose **[SSC CGL Tier-I 2014]**
(a) rhinologist (b) otologist (c) pathologist (d) podiatrist

38. To remove an objectionable part from a book **[SSC CGL Tier-I 2014]**
(a) exterminate (b) expurgate (c) extirpate (d) destroy

39. Pertaining to sheep
(a) canine (b) bovine (c) ovine (d) feline

40. Hole excavated by an animal as dwelling **[SSC CGL Tier-I 2014]**
(a) borrow (b) burrow (c) bore (d) pierce

41. Person believing in free will **[SSC CGL Tier-I 2014]**
(a) guardian (b) tyrant (c) humanitarian (d) libertarian

42. Small pieces of metal that fly out from an exploding bomb **[SSC CGL Tier-I 2014]**
(a) shrapnel (b) splinters
(c) filings (d) bullets

43. All the arts, beliefs and social institutions etc characteristic of a race **[SSC CGL Tier-I 2014]**
(a) culture (b) civilization
(c) infrastructure (d) ritual

44. The act of speaking about one's thoughts when one is alone **[SSC CGL Tier-I 2014]**
(a) silence (b) monologue
(c) dialogue (d) soliloquy

45. Passing out of use **[SSC CGL Tier-I 2014]**
(a) adolescent (b) reticent (c) translucent (d) obsolescent

Previous Years' Questions

46. A drink usually made from a mixture of one or more alcoholic drinks **[SSC CGL Tier-I 2014]**
(a) cocktail (b) mocktail (c) liquor (d) bisque

47. Affecting or relating to cows **[SSC CGL Tier-I 2014]**
(a) feline (b) bovine (c) ovine (d) vulpine

48. Something that might happen in the future **[SSC CGL Tier-I 2014]**
(a) contingency (b) insurance (c) emergency (d) prophecy

49. A special fondness or liking for **[SSC CGL Tier-I 2014]**
(a) propensity (b) inclination (c) penchant (d) preoccupation

50. Relating to kinship with the father **[SSC CGL Tier-I 2014]**
(a) patrilineal (b) fratrilineal (c) matrilineal (d) familial

ANSWERS

1 *(b)*	**2** *(d)*	**3** *(d)*	**4** *(b)*	**5** *(d)*	**6** *(d)*	**7** *(b)*	**8** *(d)*	**9** *(b)*	**10** *(b)*
11 *(c)*	**12** *(b)*	**13** *(b)*	**14** *(c)*	**15** *(d)*	**16** *(c)*	**17** *(d)*	**18** *(c)*	**19** *(b)*	**20** *(d)*
21 *(a)*	**22** *(a)*	**23** *(c)*	**24** *(b)*	**25** *(c)*	**26** *(a)*	**27** *(d)*	**28** *(b)*	**29** *(d)*	**30** *(a)*
31 *(a)*	**32** *(a)*	**33** *(a)*	**34** *(a)*	**35** *(d)*	**36** *(d)*	**37** *(a)*	**38** *(b)*	**39** *(c)*	**40** *(b)*
41 *(d)*	**42** *(a)*	**43** *(a)*	**44** *(d)*	**45** *(d)*	**46** *(a)*	**47** *(b)*	**48** *(a)*	**49** *(c)*	**50** *(a)*

SET 8

1. A part of a word that can be pronounced separately **[SSC CGL Tier-I 2014]**
(a) particle (b) sibilant (c) syllable (d) letter

2. Favouritism granted in politics or business to relatives **[SSC CGL Tier-I 2014]**
(a) monotheism (b) nepotism (c) hedonism (d) redtapism

3. A supplement to a will **[SSC CGL Tier-I 2014]**
(a) furlough (b) adjunct (c) effusion (d) codicil

4. A person who repairs broken window-glasses **[SSC CAPFs SI, CISF ASI 2014]**
(a) weldor (b) sculptor (c) glazier (d) pattisserie

5. The art of beautiful hand writing **[SSC CAPFs SI, CISF ASI 2014]**
(a) genealogy (b) calligraphy (c) cartography (d) philology

6. A co-worker in an office or institution **[SSC Multitasking Staff 2013]**
(a) companion (b) ally (c) accomplice (d) colleague

7. To supply land with water by artificial means **[SSC Multitasking Staff 2013]**
(a) irrigate (b) mitigate (c) watergate (d) postulate

8. A large burial ground **[SSC Multitasking Staff 2013]**
(a) mercenary (b) emissary (c) symmetry (d) cemetery

9. Existing only in the mind [SSC Multitasking Staff 2013]
(a) imaginary (b) fallacy
(c) gamble (d) missionary

10. Likely to arouse envy [SSC Multitasking Staff 2013]
(a) enviable (b) economical
(c) envious (d) jealous

11. One who loves and supports his or her country and is willing to defend it [SSC Multitasking Staff 2013]
(a) patriot (b) martyr (c) alien (d) atheist

12. The study of birds [SSC Multitasking Staff 2013]
(a) zoology (b) ornithology (c) physiology (d) anthropology

13. A person who readily believes others [SSC Graduate Level Tier-I 2013]
(a) credible (b) credulous (c) sensitive (d) sensible

14. Has an evil reputation [SSC LDC 2012]
(a) notorious (b) malicious
(c) magnanimous (d) dubious

15. Someone who is killed fighting for the cause of religion or faith. [SSC Multitasking Staff 2013]
(a) prophet (b) martyr (c) seer (d) mystic

16. A list of books and writings of one author or one subject [SSC Multitasking Staff 2013]
(a) biography (b) lithography
(c) bibliography (d) orthography

17. Yearly celebration of a date or an event [SSC Multitasking Staff 2013]
(a) birthday (b) jubilee (c) anniversary (d) centenary

18. A list of the names of books [SSC Multitasking Staff 2013]
(a) epilogue b) dialogue (c) catalogue (d) prologue

19. A general pardon granted by the Government to political offenders [SSC Graduate Level Tier-I 2013]
(a) excuse (b) honesty (c) amnesty d) pardon

20. A school boy who cuts classes frequently [SSC Graduate Level Tier-I 2013]
(a) sycophant (b) truant (c) martinet (d) defeatist

21. Detailed plan of a journey [SSC Graduate Level Tier-I 2013]
(a) travel kit (b) schedule (c) itinerary d) travelogue

22. Stealing of ideas or writings of someone else [SSC Graduate Level Tier-I 2013]
(a) scepticism (b) mesmerism (c) plagiarism (d) autism

23. A person who consumes human flesh [SSC Graduate Level Tier-I 2013]
(a) Savage (b) captor (c) carnivore (d) cannibal

Previous Years' Questions

24. Exclusive possession or control of anything **[SSC Multitasking Staff 2013]**

(a) monotheism (b) monopoly
(c) monism (d) mono-mania

25. Instrument that magnifies objects **[SSC Multitasking Staff 2013]**

(a) periscope (b) stethoscope
(c) telescope (d) microscope

26. Incapable of being approached **[SSC (10+2) Level Data Entry Operator & LDC 2013]**

(a) inaccessible (b) inadmissible (c) irresistible (d) illegal

27. One who takes care of a building **[SSC (10+2) Level Data Entry Operator & LDC 2013]**

(a) janitor (b) manager (c) warden (d) beadle

28. One who possesses many talents **[SSC (10+2) Level Data Entry Operator & LDC 2013]**

(a) versatile (b) unique (c) dexterous (d) attractive

29. One who lives/survives on others/other lives **[SSC (10+2) Level Data Entry Operator & LDC 2013]**

(a) expatriate (b) pesticide (c) parasite (d) refugee

30. A pole or beam used as a temporary support **[SSC Graduate Level Tier-II 2013]**

(a) scaffold (b) prop (c) lean-to (d) rafter

31. One who studies the art of gardening **[SSC Graduate Level Tier-II 2013]**

(a) agriculturist (b) horticulturist
(c) gardener (d) botanist

32. Fear of closed spaces **[SSC Graduate Level Tier-II 2013]**

(a) claustrophobia (b) aquaphobia
(c) botanophobia (d) kleptomania

33. A list of passengers and luggage **[SSC Graduate Level Tier-II 2013]**

(a) waybill (b) wagon (c) wirepuller (d) whist

34. A person difficult to please **[SSC Graduate Level Tier-II 2013]**

(a) fastidious (b) callous (c) sadist (d) ferocious

35. Study of the nature of God **[SSC Graduate Level Tier-II 2013]**

(a) philology (b) theology
(c) humanism (d) philosophy

36. A short story based on your personal experience **[SSC (10+2) Level Data Entry Operator & LDC 2013]**

(a) legend (b) anecdote (c) fable (d) parable

37. A former student of a school, college or university **[SSC (10+2) Level Data Entry Operator & LDC 2013]**

(a) genius (b) scholar (c) learner (d) alumnus

38. A building in which aircraft are housed **[SSC (10+2) Level Data Entry Operator & LDC (Nov) 2013]**
(a) granary (b) dockyard (c) garage (d) hangar

39. A person who attends to the diseases of the eye **[SSC CAPFs SI & CISF ASI 2013]**
(a) oculist (b) optimist (c) obstetrician (d) optician

40. The study of worms and insects **[SSC CAPFs SI & CISF ASI 2013]**
(a) taxidermy (b) entomology (c) ornithology (d) paleontology

41. A person who shows off his learning **[SSC CAPFs SI & CISF ASI 2013]**
(a) pedant (b) educationist (c) exhibitor (d) researcher

42. Written law of a legislative body **[SSC CAPFs SI & CISF ASI 2013]**
(a) statute (b) stature (c) static (d) statue

43. A study of sounds is known as **[SSC Graduate Level Tier-I 2013]**
(a) stylistics (b) linguistics (c) phonetics (d) semantics

44. To reduce to nothing **[SSC Graduate Level Tier-I 2013]**
(a) lull (b) null (c) annul (d) cull

45. An obviously true or hackneyed statement **[SSC Graduate Level Tier-I 2013]**
(a) syllogism (b) iconic (c) imagism (d) truism

46. Words inscribed on a tomb **[SSC Graduate Level Tier-I 2013]**
(a) epitaph (b) epitome (c) epistle (d) epilogue

47. A word composed of the first letters of the words in a phrase **[SSC Graduate Level Tier-I 2013]**
(a) abridgement (b) almanac (c) anachronism (d) acronym

48. A person of obscure position who has gained wealth **[SSC Graduate Level Tier-I 2013]**
(a) promiscuous (b) parvenu
(c) sumptuary (d) extravagant

49. Easy to shape in any desired form **[SSC Multitasking Staff 2013]**
(a) ductile (b) malleable (c) flexible (d) plasticine

50. Amount of money demanded by kidnappers **[SSC Multitasking Staff 2013]**
(a) donation (b) honorarium
(c) ransom (d) salary

ANSWERS

1. *(c)* **2.** *(b)* **3.** *(d)* **4.** *(c)* **5.** *(b)* **6.** *(d)* **7.** *(a)* **8.** *(d)* **9.** *(a)* **10.** *(a)*
11. *(a)* **12.** *(b)* **13.** *(b)* **14.** *(a)* **15.** *(b)* **16.** *(c)* **17.** *(c)* **18.** *(c)* **19.** *(c)* **20.** *(b)*
21. *(c)* **22.** *(c)* **23.** *(d)* **24.** *(b)* **25.** *(d)* **26.** *(a)* **27.** *(a)* **28.** *(a)* **29.** *(c)* **30.** *(b)*
31. *(b)* **32.** *(a)* **33.** *(a)* **34.** *(a)* **35.** *(b)* **36.** *(b)* **37.** *(d)* **38.** *(d)* **39.** *(a)* **40.** *(b)*
41. *(a)* **42.** *(a)* **43.** *(c)* **44.** *(b)* **45.** *(d)* **46.** *(a)* **47.** *(d)* **48.** *(b)* **49.** *(b)* **50.** *(c)*

Previous Years' Questions

SET 9

1. Property inherited from one's father or ancestors **[SSC Multitasking Staff 2013]**
(a) alimony (b) patrimony (c) voluntary (d) armistice

2. An apartment building in which each apartment is owned separately by the people living in it, but also containing shared areas **[SSC Graduate Level Tier-I 2013]**
(a) condominium (b) multiplex (c) duplex (d) caravan

3. A group of three powerful people **[SSC Graduate Level Tier-I 2013]**
(a) trio (b) tritium (c) trivet (d) triumvirate

4. Operation of the body after death **[SSC Graduate Level Tier-I 2013]**
(a) post-mortem (b) obituary (c) homage (d) mortuary

5. Not allowing the passage of light **[SSC Graduate Level Tier-I 2013]**
(a) oblique (b) opaque
(c) optique (d) opulant

6. Science regarding principles of classification **[SSC Graduate Level Tier-I 2013]**
(a) taxidermy (b) taxonomy
(c) toxicology (d) classicology

7. A political leader appealing to popular desires and prejudices **[SSC Graduate Level Tier-I 2013]**
(a) dictator (b) tyrant (c) popularist (d) demagogue

8. A state where no law or order exists **[SSC Graduate Level Tier-I 2013]**
(a) monarchy (b) mobocracy (c) anarchy d) democracy

9. The production of raw silk **[SSC Graduate Level 2013]**
(a) sericulture (b) seroculture (c) sariculture (d) syrumculture

10. Meaningless language with a exaggerated style intended to impress **[SSC Graduate Level 2013]**
(a) orator (b) public speaking
(c) verbalisation (d) rhetoric

11. The conference takes place once in three years **[SSC Graduate Level 2013]**
(a) tetraenning (b) triennial (c) treennial (d) thriennial

12. Talking disrespectfully of sacred things **[SSC Multitasking Staff 2013]**
(a) heresy (b) atheism (c) blasphemy (d) apostasy

13. An act of violence to take control of a plane **[SSC Constable (GD) 2013]**
(a) hold as hostage (b) abduct
(c) hijack (d) kidnap

14. One who is all powerful **[SSC Constable (GD) 2013]**
(a) omnipotent (b) omniscient (c) absolute (d) almighty

15. A form of government in which the supreme power rests with people **[SSC Constable (GD) 2013]**
(a) monarch (b) oligarchy (c) democracy (d) bureaucracy

16. Animals that live in a particular region **[SSC Constable (GD) 2013]**
(a) fauna (b) wildlife (c) native (d) beast

17. Send or bring somebody back to his own country **[SSC Constable (GD) 2013]**
(a) asylum (b) refuge (c) repatriate (d) emigrate

18. To play the part of and function as, some other person **[SSC Graduate Level Tier-I 2013]**
(a) imitate (b) pretend (c) impersonate d) act

19. To die without having made a will **[SSC Graduate Level Tier-I 2013]**
(a) intaglio (b) inveterate (c) intestate (d) insolvent

20. One who enjoys inflicting pain on himself **[SSC Graduate Level Tier-I 2013]**
(a) masochist (b) nihilist (c) egoist (d) sadist

21. Murder of a brother **[SSC Graduate Level Tier-I 2013]**
(a) fratricide (b) patricide (c) regicide (d) homicide

22. Science of human mind and behaviour **[SSC Graduate Level Tier-I 2013]**
(a) physiology (b) psychology (c) sociology (d) philology

23. A set of three related works by the same author **[SSC Graduate Level Tier-I 2013]**
(a) topology (b) trilogy (c) trichology (d) ecology

24. The study or practice of dancing or composing ballets **[SSC Graduate Level Tier-I 2013]**
(a) calligraphy (b) cartography (c) choreography (d) epigraphy

25. Having juicy or fleshy and thick tissues **[SSC Graduate Level Tier-I 2013]**
(a) succulent (b) translucent (c) dissolvent (d) dissident

26. One who thinks or speaks too much of himself **[SSC Graduate Level Tier-I 2013]**
(a) imposter (b) enthusiast (c) egotist (d) optimist

27. An exact-copy of handwriting or a picture produced by a machine **[SSC Graduate Level Tier-I 2013]**
(a) original (b) facsimile (c) copy (d) None of these

28. A person who is greatly respected because of wisdom **[SSC Graduate Level Tier-I 2013]**
(a) veracious (b) vulnerable (c) venerable (d) verger

29. An excessively morbid desire to steal **[SSC Graduate Level Tier-I 2013]**
(a) stealomania (b) kleptomania
(c) cleftomania (d) keptomania

Previous Years' Questions

30. Prohibited by law or treaty from being imported or exported **[SSC Graduate Level Tier-I 2013]**
(a) contraband (b) smuggled (c) counterfeit (d) forged

31. Intentional destruction of racial groups **[SSC Graduate Level Tier-I 2013]**
(a) regicide (b) genocide (c) homicide (d) fratricide

32. The height of an object above sea-level **[SSC LDC 2012]**
(a) altitude (b) certitude (c) latitude (d) longitude

33. One who gains benefit from something **[SSC LDC 2012]**
(a) benefactor (b) miser (c) hermit (d) beneficiary

34. A man who wastes his money on luxury **[SSC LDC 2012]**
(a) extempore (b) thrifty (c) extravagant (d) None of these

35. A man having no hair on the scalp **[SSC LDC 2012]**
(a) hoary (b) gandy (c) naked (d) bald

36. A person who pretends to be what he is not **[SSC FCI 2012]**
(a) explorer (b) prompter (c) imposter (d) diviner

37. To injure one's reputation **[SSC(10+2) Level Data Entry Operator & LDC 2012]**
(a) defame (b) ridicule (c) mock (d) agitate

38. A geometrical figure with eight sides **[SSC (10+2) Level Data Entry Operator & LDC 2012]**
(a) polygon (b) hexagon (c) octagon (d) pentagon

39. Bring about an easy and painless death for someone suffering from incurable disease **[SSC CGL Mains 2012]**
(a) euthanasia (b) strangulation (c) suicide (d) destitute

40. Fluent and clear in speech **[SSC LDC 2012]**
(a) emotional (b) enthusiastic (c) articulate (d) confident

41. The process by which a person or an organisation reduces the amount of money it spends **[SSC CGL 2012]**
(a) budgeting (b) retrenchment (c) saving (d) closure

42. An established principle of practical wisdom **[SSC CGL 2012]**
(a) marxism (b) maxim (c) neologism (d) platonism

43. Rebellion against lawful authority **[SSC (10+2) Level Data Entry Operator & LDC 2012]**
(a) mutiny (b) coup (c) revolution (d) dissidence

44. Soldiers who fight on horseback **[SSC (10+2) Level Data Entry Operator & LDC 2012]**
(a) infantry (b) artillery (c) cavalry (d) armoured

45. One who speaks for others **[SSC (10+2) Level Data Entry Operator & LDC 2012]**
(a) spokesman (b) leader (c) supporter (d) naming

46. A man who doesn't known how to read or write **[SSC (10+2) Level Data Entry Operator & LDC 2012]**
(a) uneducated (b) illiterate (c) ignorant (d) oblivious

47. An office with a salary but no work **[SSC Delhi Police SI 2012]**
(a) honorary (b) sinecure (c) insolvent (d) sinuous

48. A woman with dark brown hair **[SSC Delhi Police SI 2012]**
(a) blonde (b) philogynist
(c) brunette (d) dotard

49. Speech for the first time **[SSC Delhi Police SI 2012]**
(a) introductory speech (b) maiden speech
(c) concluding speech (d) initial speech

50. One who eats human flesh **[SSC Graduate Level Tier-I 2012]**
(a) carnivore (b) herbivore
(c) glutton (d) cannibal

ANSWERS

1. *(b)*	**2.** *(a)*	**3.** *(d)*	**4.** *(a)*	**5.** *(b)*	**6.** *(b)*	**7.** *(d)*	**8.** *(c)*	**9.** *(a)*	**10.** *(d)*
11. *(b)*	**12.** *(c)*	**13.** *(c)*	**14.** *(a)*	**15.** *(c)*	**16.** *(a)*	**17.** *(c)*	**18.** *(c)*	**19.** *(c)*	**20.** *(a)*
21. *(a)*	**22.** *(b)*	**23.** *(b)*	**24.** *(c)*	**25.** *(a)*	**26.** *(c)*	**27.** *(b)*	**28.** *(c)*	**29.** *(b)*	**30.** *(a)*
31. *(b)*	**32.** *(a)*	**33.** *(d)*	**34.** *(c)*	**35.** *(d)*	**36.** *(c)*	**37.** *(a)*	**38.** *(c)*	**39.** *(a)*	**40.** *(c)*
41. *(a)*	**42.** *(b)*	**43.** *(a)*	**44.** *(c)*	**45.** *(a)*	**46.** *(b)*	**47.** *(b)*	**48.** *(c)*	**49.** *(b)*	**50.** *(d)*

SET 10

1. One who is out to destroy the government **[SSC Graduate Level Tier-I 2012]**
(a) anarchist (b) villain (c) criminal (d) enemy

2. One who loves all mankind **[SSC Graduate Level Tier-I 2012]**
(a) philologist (b) philosopher (c) philanthropist (d) philatelist

3. A person who cannot make a mistake **[SSC Graduate Level Tier-I 2012]**
(a) inexplicable (b) inevitable (c) indispensable (d) infallible

4. Always ready to attack or quarrel **[SSC LDC 2012]**
(a) creative (b) impatient (c) aggressive (d) malicious

5. The process of deciding the nature of a disease by examination **[FCI Assistant Grade-II 2012 Paper-I]**
(a) test (b) perusal (c) diagnosis (d) operation

6. That which cannot be easily read **[FCI Assistant Grade-II 2012 Paper-I]**
(a) illegible (b) incomprehensible
(c) unreadable (d) unintelligible

7. One who finds nothing good in anything **[FCI Assistant Grade-II 2012 Paper-I]**
(a) critic (b) satirist (c) cynic (d) slanderer

Previous Years' Questions

8. In a threatening manner **[FCI Assistant Grade-II 2012 Paper-I]**
(a) ominously (b) sprightly (c) ghastly (d) terribly

9. A place of good climate for invalids **[SSC FCI Assistant Grade-III 2012]**
(a) hospital (b) asylum (c) sanatorium (d) retreat

10. To bite like a rat **[SSC FCI Assistant Grade-III 2012]**
(a) chew (b) cut (c) split (d) gnaw

11. A style in which a writer makes display of his knowledge **[SSC FCI Assistant Grade-III 2012]**
(a) ornate (b) pedantic (c) artificial (d) showy

12. Someone who performs daring gymnastic feats **[SSC FCI Assistant Grade-III 2012]**
(a) athlete (b) juggler (c) acrobat (d) conjuror

13. A list of books available in a library **[SSC FCI Assistant Grade-III 2012]**
(a) catalogue (b) bibliography (c) backlist (d) index

14. Someone who scientifically studies the birds **[SSC (10+2) Level Data Entry Operator & LDC 2012]**
(a) earthologist (b) orthopeadic (c) orthodondist (d) ornithologist

15. Something which is imagined to be real but actually does not exist **[SSC (10+2) Level Data Entry Operator & LDC 2012]**
(a) figment (b) insight (c) mirage (d) shadow

16. To officially take private property away to seize **[SSC (10+2) Level Data Entry Operator & LDC 2012]**
(a) offer (b) confiscate (c) annex (d) hijack

17. Murder of a man **[SSC (10+2) Level Data Entry Operator & LDC 2012]**
(a) regicide (b) fratricide (c) homicide (d) genocide

18. Use of force or threats to get someone to agree to something **[SSC (10+2) Level Data Entry Operator & LDC 2012]**
(a) coercion (b) Conviction (c) confession (d) cajolement

19. Animal that feeds on plants **[SSC (10+2) Level Data Entry Operator & LDC 2012]**
(a) carnivorous (b) herbivorous (c) insectivorous (d) graminivorous

20. A number of stars grouped together **[SSC (10+2) Level Data Entry Operator & LDC 2012]**
(a) orbit (b) constellation (c) solar system (d) comet

21. One who eats both vegetables and meat **[SSC LDC 2012]**
(a) omnivorous (b) vegevorous
(c) herbivorous (d) carnivorous

22. A person who studies mankind **[SSC CDO 2012]**
(a) anthropologist (b) physicist
(c) pathologist (d) philanthropist

23. Property inherited from one's father or ancestors **[SSC CDO 2012]**
(a) patrimony (b) alimony (c) voluntary (d) armistice

24. One who can not be defeated **[SSC CDO 2012]**
(a) indecipherable (b) invidious
(c) insolvent (d) invincible

25. State of anxiety or dismay causing mental confusion **[FCI Assistant Grade-III 2012 Paper-I]**
(a) constriction (b) consternation (c) concentration (d) contraction

26. To secretly store more than what is allowed **[SSC CGL 2011]**
(a) hoard (b) store (c) hide (d) aboard

27. Related to Moon **[SSC LDC 2011]**
(a) solar (b) moony (c) lunar (d) honeymoon

28. An animal story with a moral **[SSC Multitasking Staff 2012]**
(a) fable (b) tale (c) anecdote (d) parable

29. A foreigner who settles in a country **[SSC CPO SI, ASI 2011]**
(a) immigrant (b) emigrant (c) alien (d) visitor

30. Lasting only for a very short while **[SSC LDC 2011]**
(a) transparent (b) temporal (c) temporary (d) temperate

31. A raised passage way in a building **[SSC Data Entry 2011]**
(a) walkway (b) walkout (c) walkabout (d) walkover

32. Dry weather with no rainfall **[SSC LDC 2011]**
(a) summer (b) desert (c) drought (d) autumn

33. Found all over the world **[SSC LDC 2011]**
(a) international (b) universal (c) regional (d) provincial

34. One who practises one of the fine arts **[SSC LDC 2011]**
(a) painter (b) artist (c) designer (d) architect

35. A general pardon of the offenders **[SSC LDC 2011]**
(a) parley (b) amnesty (c) parole (d) acquittal

36. Strong dislike between two persons **[SSC Level Data Entry, LDC 2011]**
(a) aversion (b) antipathy (c) apathy (d) despair

37. A paper written by hand **[SSC LDL 2011]**
(a) handicraft (b) handiwork (c) manuscript (d) thesis

38. A disease which is spread by direct contact
[SSC Multitasking (Non-Technical) Staff 2011]
(a) contagious (b) infectious (c) epidemic (d) endemic

39. The study of ancient civilisations
[SSC Multitasking (Non-Technical) Staff 2011]
(a) history (b) anthropology (c) ethnology (d) archaeology

Previous Years' Questions

40. Body of singers **[SSC Multitasking (Non-Technical) Staff 2011]**
(a) coir (b) quorum (c) quire (d) choir

41. To give one's authority to another **[SSC Data Entry Operator, LDC 2011]**
(a) assign (b) delegate (c) represent (d) designate

42. One who intervenes between two or more parties to settle differences **[SSC Data Entry Operator, LDC 2011]**
(a) neutral (b) intermediary (c) judge (d) connoisseur

43. Place where wine is made **[SSC (10+2) Level Data Entry Operator & LDC 2011]**
(a) bakery (b) cloakroom (c) tannery (d) brewery

44. The art of preserving skin of animals, birds and fish **[SSC (10+2) Level Data Entry Operator & LDC 2011]**
(a) taxonomy (b) taxidermy (c) topology (d) seismology

45. A thing likely to be broken **[SSC (10+2) Level Data Entry Operator & LDC 2011]**
(a) vulnerable (b) flexible (c) brittle (d) delicate

46. Very dramatic **[SSC Graduate Level Tier-II 2011 Paper-II]**
(a) histrionic (b) hippocratic (c) hirsute (d) hoary

47. A figure of speech by which a thing is spoken of as being that which it only resembles **[SSC Graduate Level Tier-II 2011 Paper-II]**
(a) metaphor (b) simile (c) personification (d) alliteration

48. Scale used for measuring the strength of an earthquake **[SSC LDC 2011]**
(a) celsius (b) newtons (c) richter (d) linear

49. Something kept as a reminder of an event **[SSC LDC 2011]**
(a) trophy (b) souvenir (c) prize (d) antique

50. To be dogmatic in one's opinions **[SSC Stenographer (Grade 'C' & 'D') 2011]**
(a) plaintive (b) opinionated (c) undoubtable (d) secular

ANSWERS

1 *(a)*	**2** *(c)*	**3** *(d)*	**4** *(c)*	**5** *(c)*	**6** *(a)*	**7** *(a)*	**8** *(c)*	**9** *(c)*	**10** *(d)*
11 *(b)*	**12** *(c)*	**13** *(a)*	**14** *(d)*	**15** *(a)*	**16** *(b)*	**17** *(c)*	**18** *(a)*	**19** *(b)*	**20** *(b)*
21 *(a)*	**22** *(a)*	**23** *(a)*	**24** *(d)*	**25** *(b)*	**26** *(a)*	**27** *(c)*	**28** *(a)*	**29** *(a)*	**30** *(c)*
31 *(a)*	**32** *(c)*	**33** *(b)*	**34** *(b)*	**35** *(b)*	**36** *(b)*	**37** *(c)*	**38** *(a)*	**39** *(d)*	**40** *(d)*
41 *(b)*	**42** *(b)*	**43** *(d)*	**44** *(b)*	**45** *(c)*	**46** *(a)*	**47** *(b)*	**48** *(c)*	**49** *(b)*	**50** *(b)*

One Word Substitutions

SET 11

1. Intense and unreasoned fear or dislike **[SSC Stenographer (Grade 'C' & 'D') 2011]**
(a) horror (b) phobia (c) fright (d) scare

2. Excessively enthusiastic and unreasonably excited about something **[SSC Stenographer (Grade 'C' & 'D') 2011]**
(a) spirited (b) interested (c) fanatical (d) despotic

3. An agreement between two countries or groups to stop fighting **[SSC Stenographer (Grade 'C' & 'D') 2011]**
(a) compromise (b) ceasefire (c)outpost (d) protocol

4. Full of criticism and mockery **[SSC Stenographer (Grade 'C' & 'D') 2011]**
(a) discrimination (b) ridicule (c) satire (d) contempt

5. A small room in a big house, hotel, ship etc where glasses, dishes, spoons, food etc are kept **[SSC CPO SI, ASI & Intelligence Officer 2011 Paper-II]**
(a) portico (b) pantry (c) mezzanine (d) kitchen

6. List of issues to be discussed at a meeting **[SSC LDC 2011]**
(a) schedule (b) agenda (c) time-table (d) plan

7. A system of naming things **[SSC LDC 2011]**
(a) horticulture (b) miniature (c) genocide (d) nomenclature

8. Able to use left hand and right hand equally well **[SSC LDC (Nov) 2011]**
(a) ambivert (b) ambidextrous (c) ambivalent (d) ambitious

9. Speed of an object in one direction **[SSC CPO SI, ASI & Intelligence Officer 2011 Paper-I]**
(a) pace (b) tempo (c) velodrome (d) velocity

10. The place where public, government or historical records are kept **[SSC CPO SI, ASI & Intelligence Officer 2011 Paper-I]**
(a) coffer (b) pantry (c) archives (d) scullery

11. Theft of another person's writings or ideas and passing them off as one's own **[SSC CPO (SI, ASI & Intelligence Officer 2011 Paper-I]**
(a) plagiarism (b) burglary (c) piracy (d) pilferage

12. A person who has no money to pay off his debts **[SSC Combined Graduate Level Tier-I 2011]**
(a) insolvent (b) poor (c) destitute (d) pauper

13. Words uttered impiously about God **[SSC Combined Graduate Level Tier-I 2011]**
(a) amoral (b) philosophy (c) logic (d) blasphemy

14. Opposed to great or sudden change **[SSC Combined Graduate Level Tier-I 2011]**
(a) mercenary (b) conservative (c) eccentric (d) fastidious

Previous Years' Questions

15. One who compiles a dictionary **[SSC Combined Graduate Level Tier-I 2011]**
(a) geographer (b) lexicographer (c) lapidist (d) linguist

16. A test in which cells from diseased organs are removed and tested **[SSC Combined Graduate Level Tier-I 2011]**
(a) biopsy (b) autopsy (c) operation (d) amputation

17. Pertaining to cattle **[SSC Combined Graduate Level Tier-I 2011]**
(a) canine (b) feline (c) bovine (d) verminous

18. Place that provides refuge **[SSC CPO SI, ASI & Intelligence Officer 2011]**
(a) shelter (b) house (c) country (d) asylum

19. A person who gambles or bets **[SSC CPO SI, ASI & Intelligence Officer 2011]**
(a) punter (b) backer (c) customer (d) client

20. Art of writing for newspapers and magazines **[SSC CPO SI, ASI & Intelligence Officer 2011]**
(a) literature (b) journalism (c) biography (d) artistry

21. An abandoned child of unknown parents who is found by somebody **[SSC CPO SI, ASI & Intelligence Officer 2011]**
(a) foundling (b) sibling (c) urchin (d) orphan

22. Parts of a country behind the coast or a river bank **[SSC CPO SI, ASI & Intelligence Officer 2011]**
(a) swamps (b) marshes (c) hinterland (d) isthmuses

23. A written statement about someone's character, usually provided by an employer **[SSC CPO SI, ASI & Intelligence Officer 2011]**
(a) testimonial (b) memorandum
(c) certificate (d) licence

24. The highest point **[SSC CPO (Mains) 2010]**
(a) zenith (b) height (c) zeal (d) ridge

25. One who hates mankind **[Delhi Police SI, Travel & Tourism (Gwalior) 2010]**
(a) philanthropist (b) misanthropist (c) hater (d) iconoclast

26. Government by one person **[RRB Allahabad (ASM) 2010]**
(a) monarchy (b) democracy (c) oligarchy (d) dictatorship

27. A voice that cannot be heard **[SSC MT 2010]**
(a) unheard (b) faint (c) audible (d) inaudible

28. A government by the officials **[SSC (ST), SSC TA 2010]**
(a) plutocracy (b) aristocracy (c) bureaucracy (d) monarchy

29. One who cannot speak **[SSC CPO (Mains) 2010]**
(a) deaf (b) dumb (c) visionless (d) lame

30. One whose wife is dead **[Travel & Tourism (Gwalior) 2010]**
(a) widower (b) widow (c) divorcee (d) celibate

One Word Substitutions

31. One who lives for more than a hundred years **[SSC TA 2010]**
(a) saint (b) meterologist (c) demagogue (d) centenarian

32. The scientific study of living organisms **[SSC CISF 2010]**
(a) biochemistry (b) organic chemistry
(c) zoology (d) biology

33. Study of heavenly bodies **[SSC CPO (Mains) 2010]**
(a) astrology (b) astronomy (c) stargazing (d) astrophysics

34. Careful and thorough enquiry **[SSC (UDC) 2010]**
(a) investigation (b) interview (c) examination (d) exploration

35. Sudden and violent change **[SSC (GL) 2010]**
(a) cataclysm (b) catalysis (c) catacombs (d) catechism

36. Specialist in ear disease **[SSC (GL) 2010]**
(a) otologist (b) rhinologist
(c) endocrinologist (d) gerentologist

37. A movement of part of the body to express an idea or feeling **[SSC DEO 2010]**
(a) jibe (b) gesture (c) pose (d) mimicry

38. A practice of having more than one husband at the same time **[SSC (GL) 2010]**
(a) polygamy (b) polyphony (c) polyandry (d) polygyny

39. Instrument which records earth's tremor **[SSC (GL) 2010]**
(a) monograph (b) seograph (c) seismograph (d) geometer

40. The absence of law and order **[SSC MT 2010]**
(a) rebellion (b) mutiny (c) revolt (d) anarchy

41. Capable of being interpreted in two ways **[SSC (DEO) 2010]**
(a) Confusing (b) unclear (c) ambiguous (d) ambivert

42. A continuous process of change **[SSC MT 2010]**
(a) transformation (b) metamorphosis
(c) flux (d) dynamism

43. To give one's authority to another **[SSC MT 2010]**
(a) assign (b) delegate (c) represent (d) designate

44. An inscription on a tomb **[SSC (GL) 2010]**
(a) epitaph (b) crypt (c) obituary (d) legacy

45. A person living in a foreign country **[RRB (Allahabad) ASM 2010]**
(a) abroad (b) native (c) foreigner (d) remote

46. An extreme fear of being in a small confined place **[SSC (GL) 2010]**
(a) hydrophobia (b) paraphernalia
(c) claustrophobia (d) progeria

Previous Years' Questions

47. The action of looking within or into one's own mind **[SSC DEO 2010]**
(a) observation (b) examination
(c) introspection (d) introvert

48. One who intervenes between two or more parties to settle differences **[SSC MT 2010]**
(a) neutral (b) intermediary (c) judge (d) connoisseur

49. An involuntary action under a stimulus **[SSC MT 2010]**
(a) complex (b) reflection (c) reflex (d) response

50. An order requiring a person to attend a court **[SSC (GL) 2010]**
(a) courtship (b) agreement
(c) subpoena (d) command

ANSWERS

1 *(b)*	**2** *(c)*	**3** *(b)*	**4** *(c)*	**5** *(b)*	**6** *(b)*	**7** *(d)*	**8** *(b)*	**9** *(d)*	**10** *(c)*
11 *(a)*	**12** *(a)*	**13** *(d)*	**14** *(b)*	**15** *(b)*	**16** *(a)*	**17** *(c)*	**18** *(d)*	**19** *(a)*	**20** *(b)*
21 *(a)*	**22** *(c)*	**23** *(a)*	**24** *(a)*	**25** *(b)*	**26** *(d)*	**27** *(d)*	**28** *(c)*	**29** *(b)*	**30** *(a)*
31 *(d)*	**32** *(d)*	**33** *(b)*	**34** *(a)*	**35** *(a)*	**36** *(a)*	**37** *(b)*	**38** *(c)*	**39** *(c)*	**40** *(d)*
41 *(c)*	**42** *(c)*	**43** *(b)*	**44** *(a)*	**45** *(c)*	**46** *(c)*	**47** *(c)*	**48** *(b)*	**49** *(c)*	**50** *(c)*

SET 12

1. The animals of a particular region **[SSC LDC 2010]**
(a) flora (b) museum (c) zoo (d) fauna

2. An unexpected piece of good fortune **[SSC (GL) 2010]**
(a) windfall (b) philanthropy
(c) benevolence (d) turnstile

3. Clues available at a scene **[SSC LDC 2010]**
(a) circumstantial (b) derivative
(c) inferential (d) suggestive

4. An instrument for measuring the force of the wind **[Delhi Police SI 2010]**
(a) manometer (b) micrometer (c) telescope (d) anemometer

5. One who hides away on a ship to obtain a free passage **[SSC LDC 2010]**
(a) compositor (b) stoker (c) stowaway (d) shipwright

6. Practice of employing spies in war **[SSC (GL) 2010]**
(a) esplanade (b) espionage (c) espadrille (d) estrangement

7. Circular building or hall with a dome **[SSC UDC 2010]**
(a) edifice (b) palace (c) rotunda (d) spire

8. The use of many words where only a few are necessary **[SSC UDC 2010]**
(a) circumspection (b) circumlocution
(c) circumscription (d) circumvention

9. High sea waves caused by under water earthquake **[SSC MT 2010]**
(a) tsunami (b) tornado
(c) hurricane (d) cyclone

10. One who has narrow and prejudiced religious views **[SSC DEO 2010]**
(a) religious (b) fanatic (c) bigot (d) God fearing

11. A fixed territory in which authority can be exercised **[SSC (GL) 2010]**
(a) jurisdiction (b) judiciary (c) jurisprudence (d) juristic

12. To confirm with the help of evidence **[SSC DEO, DC 2010]**
(a) corroborate (b) implicate (c) designate (d) extricate

13. A noisy and bombastic speech addressed to a large assembly **[SSC (GL) 2010]**
(a) rhetoric (b)cacophony (c) harangue (d) oration

14. One who eats everything **[UP Lecturer Recruitment 2009]**
(a) herbivorous (b) gregarious
(c) credulous (d) omnivorous

15. A place where bees are kept **[SSC (A&A) 2009]**
(a) hive (b) sanctuary (c) apiary (d) aviary

16. Two words different in spelling and meaning but pronounced alike **[SSC (A&A) 2009]**
(a) homonyms (b) homographs (c) synonyms (d) homophones

17. An actor in a theatrical performance whose business is to make people laugh through his action or talk **[SSC SI Grade IV 2009]**
(a) comedian (b) joker (c) buffoon (d) acrobat

18. An abnormal fear of high places **[SSC TA 2009]**
(a) hydrophobia (b) claustrophobia (c) delusion (d) aerophobia

19. Occurring at irregular intervals in time **[SSC DEO 2009]**
(a) epidemic (b) endemic (c) temporal (d) sporadic

20. To agree to something **[SSC DEO 2009]**
(a) assure (b) assent (c) adapt (d) adhere

21. The field that studies the evolution of mankind **[SSC SI Grade IV 2009]**
(a) philosophy (b) biology
(c) anthropology (d) archaeology

22. A person who hates the institution of marriage **[UP Lecturer Recruitment 2009]**
(a) misogamist (b) pacifist (c) philogynist (d) pessimist

23. Careful in spending money **[SSC TA 2009]**
(a) punctual (b) economical
(c) miserly (d) calculative

Previous Years' Questions

24. One who breaks the law **[SSC TA 2009]**
(a) aggressor (b) politician (c) transgressor (d) pedestrian

25. Handwriting that cannot be read **[SSC DEO 2009]**
(a) ineligible (b) illegible (c) ugly (d) decipher

26. To feel or express disapproval of something or someone **[SSC DEO 2009]**
(a) declare (b) deprive (c) depreciate (d) deprecate

27. Fear of water **[SSC DEO 2009]**
(a) claustrophobia (b) hydrophobia
(c) insomnia (d) obsession

28. The belief that nothing can be known about God **[SSC A&A 2009]**
(a) agnosticism (b) theism (c) atheism (d) monotheism

29. One who sympathises with and serves the people **[SSC A&A 2009]**
(a) humanitarian (b) authoritarian (c) barbarian (d) sympathiser

30. A servile self-seeker who attempts to win favour by flattering influential people **[SSC A&A 2009]**
(a) nepotist (b) sycophant (c) psycopath (d) hedonist

31. Easily duped or fooled **[SSC DEO 2009]**
(a) insensible (b) perceptible (c) gullible (d) indefensible

32. Reproducing or memorising word for word **[SSC TA 2009]**
(a) verbatim (b) verbose (c) verbiage (d) verbalism

33. To keep a great person or event in people's memory **[SSC DEO 2009]**
(a) communicate (b) commensurate
(c) commemorate (d) commiserate

34. The tendency not to care for right or wrong **[SSC SI Grade IV 2009]**
(a) amoral (b) moral (c) immoral (d) immortal

35. Memorable recollection of the experience of one's life **[SSC SI Grade IV 2009]**
(a) biography (b) memoirs (c) testament (d) epistle

36. A person who withdraws from the world to live in seclusion and often in solitude **[SSC DEO 2009]**
(a) iconoclast (b) recluse (c) sage (d) priest

37. One who attacks and seeks to overthrow traditional or popular ideas of an institution **[SSC SI Grade IV 2009]**
(a) rebel (b) revolutionary (c) terrorist (d) iconoclast

38. That which cannot be captured **[SSC TA 2009]**
(a) unbreakable (b) ungrippable
(c) impregnable (d) slippery

39. Hard to understand **[SSC SI Grade III 2008]**
(a) punctilious (b) obtuse (c) absurd (d) abstruse

40. Inability to sleep **[SSC SOA 2008]**
(a) hysteria (b) insomnia (c) aphasia (d) amnesia

41. That which is out of place **[SSC SI Grade III 2008]**
(a) anachronistic (b) obsolete
(c) incongruous (d) archaic

42. A person who never takes alcoholic drinks **[SSC SOA 2008]**
(a) teetotaler (b) alcoholic (c) addict (d) bagpiper

43. One who journeys from place to place **[SSC TA 2008]**
(a) quack (b) cannibal (c) itinerant (d) courier

44. Dissection of a dead body to find out the cause of death **[SSC CAGC 2008]**
(a) biopsy (b) investigation (c) surgery (d) autopsy

45. Subtle difference in colour, meaning, etc **[SSC SI Grade III 2008]**
(a) nuance (b) variant (c) indifference (d) change-over

46. Government by a ruler who has unlimited power **[SSC SO 2008]**
(a) despotism (b) autocracy (c) monarchy (d) anarchy

47. Information gathering activity **[SSC SI Grade III 2008]**
(a) logistics (b) reconnaissance
(c) subversion (d) camouflage

48. An occasion of great importance **[SSC SO 2008]**
(a) exemplary (b) momentous
(c) herculean (d) grandiose

49. To have a very high opinion of oneself **[SSC SOA 2008]**
(a) exaggeration (b) adulation
(c) abundance (d) conceit

50. One who believes in giving equal opportunity to women in all fields **[SSC SOA 2008]**
(a) fanatic (b) misogynist (c) philanderer (d) feminist

ANSWERS

1 *(d)*	**2** *(a)*	**3** *(a)*	**4** *(d)*	**5** *(c)*	**6** *(b)*	**7** *(c)*	**8** *(b)*	**9** *(a)*	**10** *(c)*
11 *(a)*	**12** *(a)*	**13** *(c)*	**14** *(d)*	**15** *(c)*	**16** *(d)*	**17** *(c)*	**18** *(d)*	**19** *(d)*	**20** *(b)*
21 *(c)*	**22** *(a)*	**23** *(b)*	**24** *(c)*	**25** *(b)*	**26** *(d)*	**27** *(b)*	**28** *(a)*	**29** *(a)*	**30** *(b)*
31 *(c)*	**32** *(a)*	**33** *(c)*	**34** *(a)*	**35** *(b)*	**36** *(b)*	**37** *(c)*	**38** *(c)*	**39** *(d)*	**40** *(b)*
41 *(c)*	**42** *(a)*	**43** *(c)*	**44** *(d)*	**45** *(a)*	**46** *(b)*	**47** *(b)*	**48** *(b)*	**49** *(d)*	**50** *(d)*